7 Steps to Better Relationships

Prem P. Bhalla

GOODWILL PUBLISHING HOUSE®
B-3 Rattan Jyoti, 18 Rajendra Place
New Delhi-110008 (INDIA)

Published by:
GOODWILL PUBLISHING HOUSE
B-3 Rattan Jyoti, 18 Rajendra Place
New Delhi-110008 (INDIA)
Ph.: 25750801, 25820556
Fax: 91-11-25763428
Website: goodwillpublishinghouse.com
E-mail: goodwillpub@vsnl.net
ylp@bol.net.in

Printed at : Kumar Offset Printers, Delhi-92

Preface

Human relationships are more a matter of circumstances than of choice. One cannot choose one's grandparents, uncles, aunts or cousins. One has no choice over brothers and sisters either. It is the circumstances that create these relationships. Even the choice of relationships in school, college, society, or at the workplace is limited. One comes across people, and amongst them one builds relationships to attain one's immediate purpose in life.

The only relationships where one can exert one's choice is in selecting a spouse, or in making friends. One can also choose one's guru or mentor. With a very limited choice in building relationships, one can at best only learn how to maintain relationships.

People often wonder what makes building and maintaining relationships difficult? Why is it that even brothers and sisters born of the same parents, and educated in the same schools and colleges cannot get along? Why is it that even parents and children cannot live in harmony with each other? Maintaining good relationships with other relatives can of course be understood.

Most people claim that they have excellent relationships with some friends. Is it not surprising that while one cannot have good relationships with parents, brothers and sisters, and yet have good relationships with those who are strangers? Human beings are complex. Each person behaves differently. Everyone perceives life's situations differently. To understand human relationships, one needs to look at and understand human behaviour better.

7 Steps to Better Relationships takes you step by step into the intricacies of developing and maintaining good relationships. The book will help you understand the essentials of building relationships. The skills and abilities that are discussed can help a person enjoy better relationships at home, the workplace and in society. It guides you to understand yourself and the people around you better. You can find new happiness wherever you go.

— *Prem P. Bhalla*

CONTENTS

Building Relationships

It is natural for a man and a woman to marry and start a family. It is also natural for a couple to desire and have a child. Although this is possible only through the united effort of the couple, it is the mother who conceives and bears the child in her womb before it comes to this world.

For a child, this is the first relationship in this world—the bond between a child and a mother. The Hindu scriptures assert that a soul chooses its parents and home on the basis of one's evolution and development in the last life. Scientists tell us that a child takes form on the basis of the interaction of genes that come from the father and the mother at the time of conception. None deny that it is the mother who nurtures the child in her womb and has a deep influence upon the child.

The Hindu scriptures are emphatic on the role and the influence of the mother on the child. It is believed that the child begins to learn while still in the mother's womb. In the Hindu epic *Mahabharat*, it is said that Abhimanyu learnt the art of warfare when his father, Arjun, explained it to his mother, Subhadra, who was carrying him in her womb at that time. Since their conversation was interrupted and incomplete, Abhimanyu failed to learn the complete technique. This brought his end at the battlefield.

It is commonplace for everyone to advise expectant mothers to be happy and to have a positive attitude because of the influence on the unborn child. While doctors agree on good nutrition and care for expectant mothers, as that influences the future health of the child, there is not enough scientific evidence on the psychological influence of the mother on the unborn child. However, we cannot also ignore that many things commended by the scriptures thousands of years ago are being confirmed by the psychologists today.

The Mother

No other relationship could be as deep and meaningful to any person than that with the mother. She is not only the first person a child comes in contact with, but she is also responsible for carrying him in her womb from the point of conception until the child is fit to live and grow outside the womb. All mothers would confirm that the period from conception to childbirth is by no means easy, causing her immense hardship, but at the same time the pleasure of bringing a new person into this world is a unique experience.

After carrying a child in her womb for over nine months, the process of delivering the child is no less easy. The anxiety, the labour pains and the process of delivering the child are becoming a source of fear in the minds of many mothers-to-be who are opting for caesarian sections for easy childbirth. Doctors are complying with their requests as a part of the benefits of modern medicine.

The newly born child is a marvel. He is naked, hungry and helpless. But as an unborn child he builts a strong relationship with the mother. Soon after birth she cleans him, provides clothes and puts him to her breast to feed him. She provides him warmth and security. The child has the instinctive power to cry and draw the attention of the mother. The child is benefited. He gradually finds his way to live in this vast cruel world. In return for what he gets, he provides the mother with deep satisfaction and love. One of the finest relationships between a child and a mother is created. While the mother provides for the physical needs of the child, she is compensated through great inner satisfaction, which is difficult to describe even for a mother.

The Hindu scriptures place the mother-child relationship high above all others. In the Manu Smriti it is said: *A teacher must be respected; the spiritual teacher is worthy of ten times the respect given to a teacher; a father is worthy of hundred times the respect, but a mother is worthy of a thousand times of the respect given. Such is the importance of a mother.*

In *Mahabharat*, the Pandavas fell one by one because they could not answer the questions put to them by Yaksh guarding the lake that provided drinking water. Only Yudhistra could provide the answers and get his brothers back. When asked, "How does God ensure that He is everywhere?" Yudhistra simply answered, "Since God cannot be everywhere, he made mothers." The position of a mother is equated with that of God because she is instrumental in giving birth to a child and in preparing him to be a part of this world.

When a mother's relationship is focussed on giving, hardship and sacrifice, why do women want to become mothers? This is an instinctive need. This is the only way the human race can go on. In some cultures women are shying from becoming mothers because of cultural pressures and economic constraints. The population growth is coming down causing serious concern. This is yet another instance of mankind running away from nature.

What about those women who cannot become mothers for one reason, or another? Ask them. Many of them are desperate about it. In some cultures they are even looked down upon as incomplete or unfortunate women. This has become a specialised field in medicine and help is now available for these women through fertility clinics. Many women are now experiencing the happiness of motherhood.

Adoption offers another option to be a mother. It is common for many childless couples to adopt children from orphanages, hospitals, within the family, or amongst friends. This experience of motherhood is not complete, as the mother does not go through the process of giving birth, or experience the carrying of the child from conception until childbirth. This experience is also devoid of the pleasure of breastfeeding one's child. However, it does offer the pleasure of a mother-child relationship. Most mothers and children find happiness through this relationship, adding a new dimension to their lives.

Think it over...

It is the general rule, that all superior men inherit the elements of superiority from their mothers.

— Michelet

The Father

Next to the mother, it is the father with whom a child builds a relationship. In comparison to the mother-child bond, for obvious reasons, the father-child bond is not as strong. A deep emotional bond between the father and the mother leads to a stronger father-child relationship. A father's experience during pregnancy would be emotional rather than physical, yet bonds begin to develop with the unborn child. In some cultures, the doctors desire the husband and the wife to visit them together. They assert that a child is a joint responsibility and both must share the pleasures and pangs of childbirth together. The father is encouraged to help the wife with exercises, and he is also taught how to handle the child when he arrives. In many other cultures, besides being sympathetic and considerate, the father has little role to play until childbirth.

With many working women, childbirth is often planned as a joint husband-wife venture. Both agree to take responsibility. It is common to see fathers helping feed a child, change nappies and put the baby to sleep. In sharp contrast, there are some fathers who are not as involved, but certain bonds do develop between the child and the father.

The mother and the father play a special role in the early years of the child, and depending upon personal bonding, next to the mother, the relationship with the father is very important to the child. It has been observed that while both boys and girls build relationships with the father, girls have special affinity towards fathers and boys towards mothers.

The Grandparents

In some cultures where joint families are still prevalent, next to the parents a child begins to develop a relationship with the grandparents. In a patriarchal system, the grandparents would refer to the father's parents. It has been observed that grandparents have a special love for grandchildren perhaps because they can share mutual love and affection, and are not tied up with responsibilities as they were with their own children. It is a very special feeling, and grandparents are often accused of indulging and spoiling their grandchildren.

Little children get an opportunity to meet their maternal grandparents only when they visit them with their mother, which may not be too often, but as can be expected, the maternal grandparents indulge their grandchildren as much as the paternal grandparents. A special relationship is bound to grow between them.

While in some cultures, particularly in the developed nations where a nuclear family is the only way of living, grandparents may just be 'grandpa' and 'grandma' who visit sometimes. The relationship is much deeper in other cultures where the paternal and maternal grandparents are recognized separately. In India, the paternal grandparents are 'Dada' and 'Dadi', whereas the maternal grandparents are 'Nana' and 'Nani'.

While grandparents are often accused of indulging and spoiling their grandchildren, there are few children who get to experience the love and affection of grandparents. Though the interaction between grandparents and grandchildren is brief, yet every child has special memories of this experience because grandparents are often remembered for the enchanting stories they had narrated, or for the love they had showered in many ways. Most people are known to get nostalgic about their childhood experiences with their grandparents.

The Hindu scriptures particularly stress that everyone needs to repay their debt to their forefathers. We stand tall today because of their efforts and contribution to the society in many ways. Every individual starts from wherever the forefathers had left. One just needs to carry the torch ahead.

Uncles, Aunts and Cousins

In some cultures, uncles and aunts are just relatives connected somehow with either of the parents. Their children are just cousins. The interaction between them is limited, and the relationship is never deep.

In other cultures, as in India, where the joint family system still persists, uncles and aunts have special significance since everyone lives under the same roof, eats together from the same kitchen, and shares happiness and grief together. Since uncles and aunts are the immediate brothers and sisters of a child's mother and father, and there may be close interaction between them, the children build special relationships with them.

While in some cultures where the interaction is very limited, all bothers and sisters of the parents are described as uncles and aunts. In the joint family culture, there are separate names for uncles and aunts as related to the mother and father. The father's elder brother is addressed as 'taya', whereas the younger brother is 'chacha', and the sister is 'bhua'. The mother's brother is addressed as 'mama' and the sister as 'masi'.

Depending upon the level of interaction and personal chemistry, children develop special relationships with their uncles, aunts and cousins. Many of these relationships last a lifetime.

Brothers and Sisters

As a child grows up, a brother or sister may soon join him. Unlike the families in the past, there is a trend for smaller families. Most people desire at least two children, preferably a boy and a girl. A child's initial reaction to a younger brother or sister is that of jealousy. A child perceives competition, a sharing of mother and father. The child cannot be blamed for it because with a new child coming a mother cannot exert as much, and her attention is also diverted.

Parents are becoming conscious of this fact. To cut down upon the feeling of having to share parental love, most parents begin to prepare the child long before the baby is to arrive, and give him the feeling that the new baby would be *his* brother or sister. The father gradually encourages the child to depend more upon him than on the mother. This way the child feels fairly compensated.

When the situation is handled tactfully, most children begin to look forward to a brother or sister to play with. When the baby arrives, the child begins to take pride in him or her. No two children are alike. Even children born of the same parents, brought up in the same home and educated in the same schools and colleges turn out different. In the early years, all brothers and sisters love each other. In fact, they are protective of each other when outsiders or even parents criticize one or the other. In many cultures there are special occasions where brothers and sisters are encouraged to bond and build a good relationship. In India, brothers and sisters bond emotionally on the occasions of *Raksha Bandhan* and *Bhaiya Dooj*, festivals dedicated to the brother-sister relationship.

Friends

As the child grows up he gradually comes in contact with other children. These could be children within the home, sons and daughters of uncles, or could be children of the neighbours, or those who visit. It is not easy but a child is encouraged to share toys and play together. This is the beginning of building relationships outside family.

These friendships begin to become special when the child goes to a play school and is exposed to a group of children, and a teacher who behaves somewhat like a mother, but in reality is not the mother. The quality of these relationships is important because many of the things a child learns will be the foundation of one's attitude towards people in adult life.

The opportunities for making friends increase when one goes to a nursery school or kindergarten and then to regular school. By this time the child is aware of personal relationships. The values that the parents impart are important. Next to the parents, it is the teachers that help shape relationships. Depending upon the teacher's attitude, many children develop a strong attraction towards the teacher and what she teaches. Most teachers at the lower level are women, and because of their maternal instinct, children find it easier to learn from them.

In the school there are many children, but it has been observed that a child prefers to build a relationship only with few children. These children are attracted to each other naturally because of their temperaments. The children studying in residential schools develop deeper friendships because of greater interaction during studies, at mealtimes and also during games and free time. While the real friendships continue to be few, the number of acquaintances increases manifold. Many of these friendships go on to last a lifetime.

Many schools are now co-educational. Boys and girls study in the same class. Though in the lower classes the children are not totally conscious about it, but in adolescence the boys and the girls begin to become conscious of sexual differences and begin to take interest in the other sex. Many romances are known to have blossomed at the school level. Many students develop a crush on a teacher or another person they admire.

By the time one moves to college, one is already an adult. Being an adult does not ensure that one is mature from the point of view of building relationships. More than maturity, it is personal attraction that draws one towards the other. It is often said that at this stage boys and girls are immature and are incapable of making decisions about building relationships. However this is not true. Maturity of thought does not come from age, but from the values that the children have been taught by the parents in early years. Maturity comes from the young person's willingness to accept responsibility for ones actions, both good and bad. Such young people have a keen sense of discernment for what is right and wrong. Many children have also been observed to possess this ability. It comes from their value system.

The friendships that a child develops from childhood until one goes to college and is ready to step into the adult world, shift from person to person, from one experience to another, shaping one's attitudes towards people in general. It is during this period that one is able to experience the influence of patience, tolerance, kindness and love, and also that of greed, anger, jealousy, selfishness and suspicion. Childhood experiences make one swing between positive and negative attitudes. Again, it is the childhood value system that helps shape the personality for adult life. In the modern times, in many cultures the circumstances encourage many friendships to lead to stronger relationships than those with immediate relations like parents, brothers and sisters.

Think it over...

Real friendship is a slow grower, and never thrives unless engrafted upon a stock of known and reciprocal merit.

— *Chesterfield*

Teachers

Next to parents it is the teachers who help shape a child's attitude towards relationships. A child acts in harmony with natural instincts and the values that are imparted by the persons in his life. Parents play a crucial role to fulfil this responsibility. In joint families, the grandparents also provide a value system. In school, the teachers take over.

In the play school, the kindergarten and the primary school, lady teachers dominate the scene. They are more patient and tolerant, and with motherly instincts they are able to understand and handle children better. Besides, much is taught through rhythmic repetition of poems and songs, and lady teachers do it better. Children learn many values through stories about animals and little children. The books are appropriately illustrated. Music systems and computers have made it easier to teach little children.

Going back to what is written in Manu Smriti, it is said that a teacher must be respected. It goes on further to say that a spiritual teacher is worthy of ten times the respect. The spiritual teacher is often confused with a guru who imparts spiritual knowledge. In reality it is the regular teacher who takes on the responsibility of the spiritual teacher by teaching children simple values like truthfulness, honesty, courtesy, kindness and the willingness to share and help. When the teacher fails to provide instruction beyond the simple language or calculation skills, the teacher fails to provide value teaching. This leaves the child to learn on his own, and he may not be able to discern between right and wrong, leaving him incomplete.

From the time a child goes to a play school, and then to regular school and college, every child comes across many teachers. Ask any successful person and he or she will confirm that while success came through personal effort, but it was possible only because of the inspiration provided by some teacher, who helped kindle the spark within to gain knowledge and strive harder. There are innumerable instances when boys and girls turned around in life when a thoughtful and considerate teacher went beyond the teaching in classroom and provided guidance to get the person out of the dumps and move on the path to success.

All teachers are worthy of respect. However, it is also true that respect cannot be demanded. It must be earned. A teacher can earn respect only by providing value education that helps shape the students beyond the classroom.

With teachers leaving behind a mark on the minds of their students, it is common to have good teacher-student relationships. Many ex-students visit their teachers, particularly in residential schools, during annual day celebrations to renew past memories and also convey gratitude for the value system they learnt under their guidance in school.

God

Irrespective of the faith or religion one follows everyone sees some form of prayers or rituals within the home. This can happen very early in life, and every child is bound to ask questions leading to the existence of God. Some parents are able to explain it convincingly to the child. Many are not able to do so. When providing a value system, the parents and the grandparents draw upon stories that may also lead to the existence of a supernatural power or God. Initially, the relationship of a child with God may be superficial, or may appear to be so, but soon it becomes stronger. This is particularly so in cultures and communities where many rites, rituals and customs are followed. Many festivals are based on religion and attract the attention of children.

Children from families that pray and observe religious rituals soon develop a relationship with God. Many pray regularly. In many cultures even the younger generation observes religious customs and rituals and draws upon its relationship with God in times of need. Children who are so inclined search for religious meaning and truth in their adult life. It has been observed that people who build a relationship with God are able to adjust better in life and also take adversities in their stride.

Think it over...

Our doctrine of equality and liberty and humanity comes from our belief in the brotherhood of man, through the fatherhood of God.

— *Calvin Coolidge*

At The Workplace

After completing one's education one moves into a career. It is immaterial what career a person takes up; one needs to deal with people all the time. To ensure that one works smoothly it is necessary to maintain a cordial relationship with everyone at the workplace. This is not easy because there can be clashing interests. At the workplace there may be great competition for promotions and growth within the organisation.

The immediate relationship at the workplace is the teacher-learner relationship where one wants to learn about the structure, working and ethics of the organisation. It is essential that one must understand these facts clearly. All organisations expect the employees to follow the existing system.

The next relationship is that between a worker and the boss, who represents the senior management or the employer. One is expected to take orders from the boss and also report the progress as desired. Bosses can have whims and fancies. It is not always easy to create an ideal relationship. However, if a person knows what is to be done and fulfils the responsibilities honestly, most bosses accept it happily. Most bosses are particular about productivity and discipline within the organisation.

Since most work requires a team effort, and if the person is responsible to carry the team along in the capacity of a leader, the relationship is that of a leader and followers. In the present times the emphasis is more on teamwork than on a structure where a boss gets the work done through subordinate staff. As a member of a team one develops a sense of belongingness and strives harder to promote team productivity. Once again, it is not always easy to carry a team together because of several human factors. However, it is a part of the modern workplace structure and one needs to cope with it.

With several teams working simultaneously to perform different kinds of tasks within the organisation, there will obviously be several colleagues and one will need to have cordial relations with all of them. This sounds easy, but since all are at a similar level and proficient in their own field, besides being colleagues, they are competitors seeking to move to the next higher position. While proficiency in one's field of activity is important, very often it is the attitude towards human relationships that makes one eligible for higher positions. The ability to get along well with people is a highly rated ability. All organisations desire workers who know their way to deal with all kinds of people.

Besides the senior management, the colleagues and the teammates in the organisation, there are a whole lot of other people one needs to deal with. In any organisation there would be customers, or the people who benefit directly from the operations of the organisation. Whether they are customers, or in some way beneficiaries of the organisation, they can be sensitive about the service they get. Since there could be some deficiencies that are beyond control, the remedy lies in building good relationships. These can smoothen out the wrinkles whenever a problem surfaces.

Suppliers are equally important to an organisation. They keep the organisation in operation. If the supplies were to stop, the purpose of the organisation would fail. Therefore, cordial relationships with the suppliers are as important as those with customers. Most organisations buy shrewdly, and this is possible only through good relationships. Getting the right deal can greatly influence the purpose and profitability of an organisation.

Most organisations have yet another class of people they need to cope with. One does not get to see them because they may be living faraway. These are the people who make enquiries and deal with the organisation through the written word. These people will write letters, send fax messages or get in touch through e-mail. They are as important as the customers and suppliers who come in person. One needs to build an equally effective relationship with them. This requires good writing skills. Many organisations follow a set style in responding through written communications.

Since the telephone services in many parts of the world are effective, many of the suppliers or customers may prefer to get in touch with the organisation through telephone. Therefore, communicating well verbally is important to build good relationships with people.

Coming around a full circle one finds that the learning experience in an organisation does not end with the initial learning when one joined the organisation. All organisations are forever evolving and moving into new directions. This has become possible through knowledge explosion. One needs to be in constant touch with the latest. To make this possible most organisations have in-house training programmes. A good teacher-learner relationship goes a long way in fulfilling this important need.

The Society

Relationships within the home and at the workplace are not all in life. There are many people we meet every day. We cannot call them relatives, friends or colleagues, but nonetheless they play a role in our lives. Good relationships with them can make life smooth and comfortable. Many of us walk out of our flats to use the lift to reach the ground floor. The liftman takes us up and down making life easy. A simple smile can make his day. In the same way the building guards, the gardeners and support staff that help maintain the building expect an occasional "thank you". A smile or a greeting gratifies them easily.

Even in the market it is not only the proprietors of the stores we visit frequently but also the staff that expect courtesy and a smile. It has been observed that when the relationships are good one gets better service. The situation is no different in restaurants, clubs and other public places. It is always beneficial to maintain good relationships at every level. People gradually get to know you, and provide better service. Many visit the parks and other places during a morning or evening walk and build relationships with others who frequent the place at the same time. It is human nature to meet each other and develop relationships. The bonds may not be very deep unless some of these relationships transform into friendship, but cordiality is always remembered and helps contribute to one's personality and character.

Membership in clubs offers a great opportunity of knowing a lot of people. Those who make friends easily aspire for offices in clubs and other organisations in the society. This is possible only through good relationships.

Those who hold positions in public life build relationships with very large groups of people known to them initially only as acquaintances. Good relationships help maintain one's position in society.

Think it over...

To study mankind, is not learning to hate them; far from such a malevolent end, it is learning to bear and live easily with them.

— *Shakespeare*

The Spouse

As a child grows up, it becomes aware of the opposite sex. However, it is only during adolescence that one becomes conscious of the sexual urge and attraction towards the opposite sex. A few relationships blossom towards the end of school, but most of them develop in the college. Some even lead to marriage. In conservative families where people still believe in arranged marriages, friendships are not too deep, and the selection of the spouse is left to the parents and senior relatives.

The institution of marriage has undergone great changes in the past few decades. While those who have enjoyed good marital relationships confirm that the husband-wife relationship is the most sublime of all relationships, those with failed marriages feel that nothing could be worse. Much depends upon individual attitudes and commitment to the relationship. Much of it comes from the parents and the values that a culture believes in.

While in some cultures marriage is only a union between a man and a woman, who build a family through the relationship, in some cultures marriage is a union between two families who stand with each other in good and bad times. In such circumstances, both the husband and the wife get a new set of parents-in-law, grandparents, uncles, aunts and cousins, and depending upon personal temperaments and circumstances many new relationships develop after marriage. Some of these are challenging relationships, as we have all seen. But when one learns to cope with them, they are equally rewarding.

Think it over...

If you would have the nuptial union last, let virtue be the bond that ties it fast.

— Rowe

Special Relationships

Besides the many relationships that we have discussed, one cannot ignore that there are other kinds of relationships as we see amongst pen friends, who may never have met each other and yet enjoy a special relationship. These friendships have gradually changed into friendships on the Internet that make them a lot better than just being pen friends. Many of these friendships have led to marriages.

There are other kinds of relationships also, as between two adults of the opposite sex who find great pleasure in each other's company but may not get married. Both of them may be unmarried, divorced or even be a widow or widower, or be a combination of these. They may or may not be physically involved with each other. The pleasure they derive makes the relationship very important to both of them, even though the society may not look upon it kindly sometimes. What compels people to develop these relationships is difficult to assess. In each case the circumstances and reasons could be different.

Gurus and Mentors

In some religions and faiths it is common for people to accept a guru or a mentor to guide them both in religious and general values of life. Many people adopt an attitude of subservience to the guru and follow instructions to the word. Some of these relationships are deep and abiding, but may or may not involve the whole family. Nothing comes without a price. Many pay for the relationship in one form or another. Some do it as a status symbol. When people use this relationship to become better persons and find greater happiness in day-to-day life, it is then worthwhile to have a good guru or spiritual guide.

Points to Ponder...

- One begins to build relationships even before birth.
- The relationship with the mother is the most binding of all relationships.
- Next to a mother, a father provides values that influence relationships.
- Grandparents and grandchildren are known to have special affinity for each other.

- One learns interpersonal skills sooner in the atmosphere of a joint family.
- Children born of the same parents, brought up in the same home and school could be different.
- One builds relationships outside the home through friends.
- Teachers play a definite role to shape one's attitude towards relationships.
- In some cultures one develops a relationship with God at an early age.
- To succeed at the workplace one needs to build a variety of relationships.
- Good relationships in society make life smooth and comfortable.
- Marital relationships can be heavenly or hellish.
- There is no end to the kind of relationships one can build in different circumstances.

What Makes Relationships Difficult?

Most of the relationships are created by circumstances and not by choice. Some believe that a soul has a choice to choose one's parents. Since there is no scientific evidence to confirm this, one can only accept that one cannot choose one's parents. One has no choice over brothers and sisters either. One cannot also choose one's grandparents, uncles, aunts or cousins. All of these are immediate relatives. The circumstances automatically create these relationships.

One does not have control of choice with relationships in school, at college, the workplace, or in society. Everywhere one comes across people, and out of necessity one builds relationships to attain one's immediate purpose in life. One chooses the best amongst the many.

The only relationships where one can exert one's choice is when selecting a spouse or friends. In some cultures where marriages are still arranged, even that choice is handled by the parents and not by the concerned persons. One can, of course, choose one's own guru or mentor if one wants to.

It is obvious that one has very limited choice in building relationships; most of them are just a part of the family as a whole. One cannot choose relatives. One can at best only learn how to maintain relationships. This is not an easy exercise because maintaining relationships requires one to be in harmony with the other persons, and human nature being what it is, creating this harmony is very difficult. Since human beings are gregarious and desire to build good relationships, sometimes out of frustration, people adopt deviant behaviour. We see people taking on a mistress, or even lesbian or gay partners.

People often wonder what makes building relationships difficult? Why is it that even brothers and sisters born of the same parents, and educated in the same schools and colleges cannot get along? Why is it that very often even the parents and the children cannot be in harmony with each other? The difficulty in having good relationships with other relatives can of course be understood. Yet many people claim that they have excellent relationships with some friends. Is it not interesting that although one doesn't have good relationships with one's parents, brothers and sisters yet have good relationships with strangers? Human beings are complex. Each person behaves differently. Everyone perceives life situations differently. To understand human relationships, one needs to look at and understand human behaviour better.

Everyone is Different

In general, people may be fair or dark, tall or short, slim or plump, and may have varied characteristics. Yet on the whole they appear similar. This misleads a person to think that the same kind of behaviour with people would produce similar results. This is not true. In some ways people may seem to respond the same way, but the basic truth is that everyone is different.

Every person is born unique. The genetic setup of an individual depends upon the genes of the chromosomes, half of which come from the mother, and the other half from the father. Since there are millions of cells involved, and each carries genes of different characteristics, it is obvious that the person born is bound to be unique. After birth each child is exposed to different environments. Each child responds differently. Each child grows with different thoughts and perceptions. With such variables can two people be alike? Even when two persons look alike, as we see amongst identical twins, yet they are different in their thoughts, perceptions and habits. They respond differently to the same situation.

According to the Hindu scriptures it is believed that every person brings with him or her fruits of the past lives. A person chooses parents and a home in harmony with the personal evolvement in the past lives. It is explained that since the past lives of each person was different, the brothers and sisters born of the same parents, brought up in the same home, and studying in the same schools and colleges are completely different. Scientists do not accept anything without a valid proof. To convince them, modern psychiatrists practicing hypnotism have been able to get information about the past lives of patients. It has become possible to connect present-day problems of people with past lives, confirming that each person is unique.

Millions of people have come to this world and gone. Not one was like the other. There are millions of people living today, but not one of them is like the other. Even in the days to come, no two people would be alike. We need to understand that people may appear to be similar, but each one is different from the other. Why should we then look at them as though they are similar? Why should we use the same yardstick to measure all people? When people are different, why should they not be accepted as such?

When learning to build better relationships a person needs to accept that all people are different. Everyone must be treated as an individual. We cannot generalize our relationships with everyone. No one common method is good for all people. Nothing hurts people more than not being treated as an individual. A person who desires to build good relationships needs to remember this sentiment at all times.

Think it over...

Man is to be trained chiefly by studying and by knowing man.

— Gladstone

Everyone is Right

Another important aspect of human nature is that everyone holds different views about various things, and from his or her point of view, whatever a person says or does is right. This is very difficult for most people to accept. However, it is absolutely true. A person's behaviour is based upon what he or she was taught, and whatever one learnt and experienced in life. If a person has always lived amongst animals, can one behave like a human being? Observe children. They will copy whatever they see in their homes. They will speak the same language. They will adopt the same behaviour. Have you observed that people from different areas speak in a particular style and language? This explains the variety of dialects we have in the same language. Despite the prescribed phonetics even an international language like English is spoken in a variety of ways. It has been observed that people coming from different regions and backgrounds have similar accents. To them, that is the right way to pronounce words.

Observe the eating habits. People from different regions and backgrounds adopt different eating habits and behaviour. People behave in harmony with what they are taught. It would be a mistake to label any response that is based upon learning as wrong. From the person's point of view it is right.

When a person desires to build good relationships with people, it is necessary that one understands that from an individual's point of view he or she is right. In such circumstances one must accept whatever a person speaks or does as right, until such time that one can convincingly persuade the other person to understand that there are better ways of saying and doing the same thing. This is not easy because when we suggest a different way, we expect the person to change one's perspective about something. Change involves uncertainty. People are afraid to accept change because it means stepping out of one's comfort zone. This makes creating and maintaining relationships with people difficult. This aspect offers a challenge to everyone. A person must first be accepted with whatever thoughts, perceptions and habits one has, and then gradually be motivated to accept that there are better ways of doing the same things.

People are Sensitive

Just as people are different and are right in thinking and looking at situations in harmony with what they know and have experienced, another aspect that needs the attention of persons who desire to build good relationships is that people are sensitive to certain issues. One must be aware of these sensitivities when speaking to other people. When these sensitivities are ignored, people get turned off and one fails to develop a good relationship.

Every person is instinctively guided by three basic needs. The first is self-preservation. Everyone desires security. This is possible through good health, a useful vocation and means to live honourably. The second need is to keep one's race going. This is possible through a spouse and family. The third need is for power. People desire recognition and respect. Money plays an important role to fulfil this need. It is common to see people obsessed with money. It makes them ignore other needs. We see it all the time in everyday life.

One would think that it is easy to avoid touching the sensitivities of people on these issues, but it is not so. Human needs are manifested in small day-to-day activities. Although different activities can be classified under one or the other need, it is difficult for a person to appreciate the finer sensitivities pertaining to an activity in other people. One learns about these sensitivities only through experience. Since experience is gained slowly, one can learn to build and maintain good relationships only with time.

During one's efforts to build relationships one must always be careful about human sensitivities. When gaining experience and understanding about individual peculiarities, it is possible that one may unintentionally touch a sensitive point in others. In such an event the best thing to do is to say "sorry". Seeking an apology hurts the ego at that particular time, but for a person who believes in good relationships, this is the easiest way to get over the problem and move ahead. An immediate apology heals the injury and is soon forgotten. Through experience it has been possible to identify some common sensitivities and ways to avoid them. Let us consider some of them.

The Name

Most people are very sensitive about the way their name is pronounced or spelt. One may argue that people have strange names. With millions of combinations, the people around the world make it very difficult to do full justice to names without having learnt the correct pronunciation or spelling. However, people everywhere are sensitive about their names.

Considering the sensitivity of the people in relation to their names, newspapers and magazines use different names even when reporting true stories and incidents. The purpose is to highlight an incident and not hurt any individual. In the same way, we see a statement that precedes serials and movies. It warns that any resemblance of names and situations is coincidental, and has no bearing with any persons, living or dead. Since these serials are watched by millions of people, and there are bound to be some similarities, the producers want to stay clear in the event some sensitivity is touched.

When building good relationships, one cannot afford to ignore this sensitivity in people. When it is necessary to interact with people, one must learn to pronounce the names correctly. In written communication the spellings must be right. People can also be sensitive about over-writing of names in letters and on envelopes. People in high positions like their position or title to be mentioned with their name. This is a human sensitivity everyone must be careful about.

Think it over...

To live is not to live for one's self alone; let us help one another.

— *Menander*

Special Occasions

Many people are sensitive about special occasions and milestones in their lives. Have you ever observed how people take offence when relatives and associates forget occasions like birthdays, wedding anniversaries or special celebrations pertaining to their families? People expect to be greeted on special successes, promotions and recognitions. In the same way, people also expect friends and associates to express feelings of condolence in moments of grief and bereavement.

When it is desired to build good relationships, it is necessary that one does not offend people on this account. It would be advisable to maintain the details month-wise so that greetings can be conveyed appropriately and in time. When a person frequently interacts with people, it becomes easy to remember the names and specialties of people. In this way a person soon builds lasting relationships.

Think it over...

People will forget what you said, people will forget what you did, but people will never forget how you made them feel.

— *Anon*

Family Priorities

Family priorities vary in different cultures and countries. In many developed countries, the economic freedom has corroded family values, and family ties are weak. In several Asian countries the family ties are strong, and the joint family pattern exists. Whatever be the level of priority, everyone is sensitive about family ties. They motivate people to go to great extremes to ensure family welfare and security. For the sake of love and care people make great sacrifices. Many still give higher priority to family ties than to their material possessions.

People are very sensitive about matters pertaining to his or her family. To every individual, family ties are important because that is the basis of his or her existence. Lives rotate around families. The entire society is built on the institution of home. Every person desires his or her family to be secure and their needs met. People will go to great lengths to achieve their family goals. To them, this goal is top priority.

To build good relationships one needs to remember that the family is an important priority for everyone. One must always honour these family ties.

Personal Priorities

People often go out of the way to please others to build good relationships with them, and wonder why they are not as congenial as they would like them to be. The simple reason is that they may have different priorities. This may not happen too often, but does happen occasionally.

This can be very frustrating to a person who makes special efforts to build good relationships. Very often people lose their patience. This would be as bad as when the other person is more responsive to another priority. There is no use in being frustrated or losing one's patience. The other person may have his or her reasons to have another priority. It could be important. If so, it would need to be respected in the interests of future relationships. To build good relationships, it is important to understand the compulsions of others and to accept them gracefully. That helps generate goodwill.

A Personal Philosophy

Another aspect that makes building good relationships difficult is that every person is guided by what people call 'a personal philosophy'. The word 'philosophy' is derived from the Greek word *'philosophia'* meaning 'love of wisdom'. A personal philosophy refers to an attitude that guides one's behaviour. It pertains to the fundamental nature or the way one looks at knowledge, reality and existence. When every individual is unique, the way one looks at life is bound to be different. One's personal philosophy has much to do with the attitude or the way of looking at life and relationships. Under such circumstances, it is bound to create obstacles for building good relationships. It is therefore important that a person must understand that crossing this hurdle is not easy. One would be wise to accept people as they are and not be frustrated by such problems.

Inconsistent Behaviour

After having dealt with a person for sometime one would tend to believe that one knows enough about the person. With this knowledge, one would believe that it should be easy to build good relationships. However, it does not happen like that. No knowledge about any person is sufficient. The truth is that people do not always behave consistently. Life is dynamic. It is forever ushering in changes. In responses to these changes people alter their attitudes and activities. People behave differently depending upon the occasion.

Have you ever observed a crowd or a mob? Have you noticed how irrationally they may behave? They may even get violent. You may be led to think that the crowd or the mob consisted of unreasonable people. No, it is not so. Most of the people may really be good people in everyday life. The truth might be that the immediate circumstances had provoked them to behave in an irrational way. Later, they may even repent their behaviour. Human beings are so built that they can act inconsistently at times.

One can also observe inconsistency in human behaviour when we find extremes of behaviour amongst most people. Have you noticed that when a person has an occasion to be happy, the person goes overboard in expression of this happiness? In the same way, when a person is faced with difficult circumstances, again one goes to the extremes to be utterly dejected. One forgets that both the conditions are transient. Both have a place in every person's life. Yet they only come and go. A balanced person takes both the conditions in the normal stride. One must accept them as part of life.

Another reason for inconsistent behaviour is that everyone is busy keeping up with the others. The present day society is so tuned that nobody likes to be left behind. At the same time, people want to conform to others lest they might be thought of as inferior in some sort of way. Nobody likes to be thought of as inferior or lacking in any way. Therefore they strive to conform to others even though the activity may not be in harmony with their personality.

Think it over...

There are depths in man that go to the lowest hell, and heights that reach the highest heaven, for are not both heaven and hell made out of him, everlasting miracle and mystery that he is.

— *Carlyle*

Different Perceptions

If a group of people were to sit around in a circle and draw the image of an object placed in the middle of the circle, the drawing of each person would be different from the others. The reason is obvious. Everyone sees the object from his or her point of view and draws it accordingly. This is exactly what happens when several people look at different situations in everyday life. Everyone sees it from his or her angle, or views it with one's own perception. For obvious reasons the perceptions of people are likely to be different.

It is not only that people would have different perceptions. What confounds the situation further is that perceptions are always changing with changing circumstances. Have you observed the marked difference in perception in the way your parents handled you when you were a child, and now when you are an adult, how you deal with your children? Have you noticed how the relationship between a husband and wife alters with time? Perceptions change with experience and maturity. Like all other things perceptions keep changing and influence relationships accordingly.

Perception and Knowledge

People would normally perceive situations and circumstances on the basis of their knowledge. This would only be natural. However, it has been observed that there is a gross difference between people's perception and knowledge.

Perception refers to one's ability to see, hear, or become aware of something through senses. It would also mean to be able to understand the true nature of something. Some also call it insight. On the other hand, knowledge refers to information and skills gained through education or experience. Human nature is such that it is not easy to develop harmony between perception and knowledge. While knowledge based upon experience should be the guiding factor, the senses that control perception tend to pull one's thoughts towards a direction that gives greater pleasure to the person. One is easily attracted to what is pleasurable rather than what is reasonable. In view of such circumstances, Confucius has rightly warned, "To see what is right and not do it, is want of courage, or of principle."

A person trying to build relationships should always be aware that an individual's perception might not be in harmony with one's knowledge.

Other Influences on Behaviour

We have observed that people are born different; they grow up to have a personal philosophy or way of looking at life. We have also seen that while people are personally sensitive to certain things, yet they always feel that they are right. We have also observed that people look at things differently and one's perception might not always be based on personal knowledge. All these make building relationships with people difficult. But this is not all. There are several other influences that affect the way people behave.

Some of these influences are beyond control. For example, there is the influence of one's destiny, or fate, which is beyond control. There are some influences that can be controlled by a person if he or she wants to, but having once become a habit, it is invariably difficult to alter the habit without persistent effort. Most people are poor listeners. They are more comfortable talking than listening. This can be corrected, but not without determination and serious effort. Let us look at some of the other influences that affect human behaviour, making it difficult to build relationships.

Biorhythms

Biorhythms refer to a recurring cycle in the functioning of an organism. Human beings, animals and even plants experience these changes. A common example is the everyday cycle of staying awake and sleeping when we experience day and night. Even this experience is altered with the changes in weather and climate. Biorhythms reflect rhythmic change that affects the physical state and activity patterns of plants and animals. The seasonal changes cause hibernation and also influence breeding and migratory patterns in animals, and flowering in a variety of plants. The variation in the length of the day causes hormonal changes, and these influence the physiology of plants and animals.

One can observe these changes when a person travels swiftly in a jet plane into areas with different timings and sleeping and waking patterns. The biological changes are described as 'jet lag', and it takes some time before the body gets adjusted to the new environments and timings.

The circadian rhythm affecting the metabolic rhythm is based on the changes in the 24-hour day, and is found in most living beings. These affect the body temperature, blood pressure, the level of energy, attentiveness, appetite, sleeping and waking patterns, and many other activities. The moods also follow a set rhythm. The heart too beats to a rhythm. The menstrual cycle in women, and the sex drive in both men and women are also controlled by these rhythms. The sleeping and waking patterns are also influenced by biorhythms. In sick people, the body temperature, blood pressure and the pulse are recorded at fixed times each day to observe these changes.

The body temperature in human beings is lowest between 4.00 and 6.00 a.m. It increases gradually by mid-morning, and one experiences a higher level of energy. Those who sleep late and also rise late experience increase in energy levels later in afternoon. Efficiency varies with the biorhythms. These vary from one person to another. Only the person concerned can assess levels of energy at different times of the day. Taking advantage of this fact, people prefer to do the difficult and challenging assignments when the efficiency is at a peak, and the routine jobs can be handled at other times.

Since moods are influenced by biorhythms, and relationships can be made or marred because of one's mood, the knowledge of biorhythms can be useful when one sets out to build relationships.

Think it over...

Man is an animal, which alone among animals refuses to be satisfied by the fulfilment of animal desires.

— *Alexander Graham Bell*

Hormones

A hormone is a chemical messenger that stimulates action. A hormone is a substance produced by a living thing and carried by blood in animals and by sap to specific cells or tissues in plants. The purpose is to stimulate action. The word 'hormone' has been derived from the Greek word *'hormōn'* meaning 'setting in motion'. A variety of hormones are secreted by ductless glands situated in different parts of the body and render very useful service. The ductless glands as a group of body organs are referred together as the endocrine system.

The hypothalamus, which is no bigger than the tip of the thumb, along with the pituitary gland rules the entire endocrine system. When a person has not eaten anything, the level of blood sugar falls. It is then that the hypothalamus creates the desire to eat. When the weather is hot, it adjusts the internal thermostat. The thyroid controls the body metabolism just as the parathyroid controls the level of calcium in the blood. The pituitary and the pineal glands regulate sexual development. The pancreas controls insulin. The ovaries in women and the testes in men influence sexual activity. There are as many as 200 hormones that activate the biological functions.

While the biorhythms influence the secretion of hormones with change of time, weather and climate, the secretion of the hormones is also influenced by personal situations and circumstances. For example, when you are travelling in a car that goes out of control and an accident is imminent, the hypothalamus signals the release of adrenaline which prepares the body for fight or flight. The heart beats faster, breathing becomes deeper, the pupils dilate to improve vision, the perspiration cools the body, and face turns pale with fear. This is due to the blood vessels contracting to prevent possible bleeding.

While the hormones influence one's mood and temperament, one cannot control their release in the body. Since the release depends upon personal sensitivity to particular situations, and this can vary immensely. The release of hormones varies, and with it the interaction in human relationships. Since women are greatly influenced by the changes during the menstrual cycle and men by their own set of hormones, couples experience wide variations of acceptance and rejection in marital relationships. To a lesser degree the hormones also affect other relationships.

Maya

While modern scientists describe the varying behaviour of people because of biorhythms and influence of hormones, the Hindu scriptures describe it because of

Maya, which is a mystical control of an individual by God through unexplainable influences. Some describe these influences as illusions or deceptions. Others explain that these arise because of ignorance. However, the Hindus insist that no one is above the influence of *Maya*.

In the *Ramcharitmanas* there are several references to *Maya*. The sage Visvamitra had requested Sri Ram and Lakshman to protect his *yagna* in the forest. With the completion of the *yagna*, the sage guided both the brothers to Mithila. On the way Sri Ram relieved Ahalya from the curse of her husband, and later, though Sri Ram broke Shiva's bow and was to marry Sita, all the four brothers were married to four sisters, uniting two powerful families. What else could it be if not the grace of the Lord?

In the *Ramcharitmanas*, Uttar-kand, Doha 62A, it is said, "*Maya* deluded even Garuda who is foremost amongst the Lord's devotees and is an enlightened soul. How can the common people be immune to it?" In Bal-kand, Doha 117, it is said, "Just as a sea shell appears as though made of silver, and a mirage gives the impression of water, what we see are delusions. Nobody can dispel them." In Uttar-kand, Doha 41, it is explained, "Listen, brother, the good and the bad qualities that we see are because of *Maya*. The greatest wisdom is to accept them as illusions. To accept them as real is ignorance."

Maya refers to the illusions that we perceive in everyday life. They are beyond human explanation. Does it matter if God's *Maya* is real or illusory? The person who has good relationships to build should know that nothing is possible without the grace of God.

Destiny

Very close to the concept of *Maya* is the concept of destiny controlling the affairs of mankind. Destiny refers to the hidden power believed to control what will happen in the future. The Hindus firmly believe that at the time of birth a person brings forth the fruits of past lives. The deeds of this life pave the way for what awaits one in the future.

The role destiny plays is clearly apparent from the *Ramcharitmanas*, which describes the way things took shape just when Sri Ram was to be crowned as the King of Ayodhya. In less than a day, a maidservant was successful in changing the history of the kingdom. Instead of the crown, Sri Ram got fourteen years of exile. Could the maid have done it without the will of the Lord? It is strange how destiny works. In the *Ramcharitmanas*, Ayodhya-kand, Doha 77, it is said, "One commits the offence, but another reaps the fruit. Strange are the ways of God. No one can understand them." Bal-kand, Doha 159B describes it this way. Tulsi Das says, "Circumstances gradually build up for whatever has to happen. Either the circumstances come to a man, or take him to the cause of the doom." Ayodhya-kand, Doha 171, reads: Vashistha said, "Bharat, fate is very powerful and compelling. Profit and loss, life and death, fame and infamy– these are controlled by destiny."

Destiny has a definite role to play in the lives of all people. Some accept the circumstances by saying that it is the will of God. Others use the circumstances as an opportunity to use their skills and abilities to set right their life today so that they may enjoy a better tomorrow.

Lack of Listening Skills

It is difficult to develop relationships with people for yet another important reason. People lack listening skills. This is equally applicable to both the parties. People prefer to speak rather than listen. Everyone feels that they have a valid viewpoint, and they must express it. Everyone desires to be listened and not be spoken to. People are poor listeners because a person's listening speed is almost four times the speaking speed. Since only one-fourth of the listening ability is used, while the other person is talking, one's mind drifts elsewhere to respond to the person who is speaking, or strays somewhere else altogether.

Before one can learn to build good relationships, one must learn to be a good listener. When several people hear the same thing, it is not necessary that everyone's response to the message would be the same. Several factors influence the listening process. Noise may not permit a message to be heard correctly. To a bored person whatever is being said may not sound attractive. People with mental blocks may not respond favourably to certain ideas. A restless person may interrupt the speaker and not get the correct message. An individual's receptivity could be low because of fatigue. Under such circumstances one can easily understand why good listening skills are important in building good relationships.

Acting Judgmental

Another reason why it becomes difficult to build relationships is that people are judgmental. They are excessively critical of people and things. Have you observed how children could be critical of their own parents? How people blame others for their own failings? People will blame the government, the civic authorities, their relatives, the weather, etc. without once realizing that they too are a part of the system. Just as they are critical about others, people would be critical about them. When people find fault easily, it is not possible to build a relationship. This is a common characteristic found in most people.

It is possible to build good relationships only when one appreciates others and not criticize them. Everyone needs to remember this simple rule.

Points to Ponder...

- Most relationships are created by circumstances and not by choice.
- People may look alike, but everyone is different in response and behaviour.
- From one's own point of view everyone is right in word and action.
- People's sensitivities need to be respected.
- Everyone is sensitive about one's name, family, life and priorities.
- People live with an undefined personal philosophy of life.
- It is human nature to respond and act inconsistently.
- Everyone perceives situations differently. Their perception may not be in harmony with their knowledge.
- Besides personal thoughts, people are controlled by unseen influences like biorhythms, hormones, *Maya* and destiny.
- Most people lack listening skills.
- Being judgmental prevents people from building good relationships.

Relationships Within The Home

A home is the basic institution on which the foundation of a society is established. A cluster of homes forms a village or a colony; colonies together form a town or a city. Together all these form a nation.

A structure of wood, bricks and mortar is just a house. It is the people who live in the house who convert it into a home, a place where one grows and builds memories. Each home, small or big, has its own characteristics depending upon the people who reside within it. While some homes feel cold and dreary, others are inviting, warm and cosy.

A home is where the heart is. Deep emotional bonds are built within the precincts of a home. Relationships too are made or unmade within the home. Irrespective of what a person does for a career, or wherever he or she goes in the day, it is only the home where one returns each day to recoup lost energy, recharge one's battery and prepare for another day.

It is within the home that a man and woman develop intimacy and raise a family. The children are born and everyone gets together to share the joys and sorrows of everyday life. Grandparents, father, mother, uncles, aunts and cousins interact within the home, teaching one another about better relationships. Much is learnt and experienced through these interactions, preparing one for other kinds of relationships outside the home.

Good relationships just do not happen. They need to be created through love, care and understanding. A variety of inputs are required for different relationships even within the home. Let us take a look at them and see how one can enjoy each relationship.

Making of a Home

The tough competitive life of the modern times compel many single persons to set up a home alone, settle down in a vocation, marry and the wife moves into the husband's home. In rare cases a man may move in to live with his wife. In many cultures it is said that a bachelor's home is just a camp. It becomes a home only when the wife moves in after marriage. In many cultures women are as economically independent as men and spend a full day working at a vocation. Despite the fulltime involvement in a career, the home is built more through the finer touches of women than men.

Although more marriages are failing today than ever before, the children are a great binding and motivating force in a marriage. Through children the parents relive their own childhood, providing the children toys that their parents could not afford to give them, buying them comfort, a better education and all that they missed as children. Bringing up children is a complex responsibility. Though the parents will insist that they have done the best any parent can do, results vary from one situation to another. One thing that cannot be denied is that it is within the home that memories are made, and the foundation of one's happiness in life is laid.

Intimate Relationships

Relationships within the home are marked with physical and emotional intimacy. They are invariably informal and friendly, and the family members are closely involved. For this reason they are often referred to as intimate relationships. These relationships are characterized by feelings of love, caring and sharing. The family members are attached to each other.

It is not easy to explain or describe it, but mutual love is an essential ingredient of intimate relationships. Love, as a feeling, is much deeper than just liking one another. It would, however, include companionship when people like to be in each other's company. When love is passionate, it may lead to physical symptoms like increased heartbeat and shortness of breath. In some cases the feeling may lead to sexual relations. It is interesting to observe that cultural and regional differences influence the nature of love and intimacy.

People develop intimate relationships for several reasons. Instinctive attachment, as between a mother and a child, or a father and a child is natural. In a materialistic world, a common reason is the need for security. People live together to feel more secure. This is an easy way to get over one's fear of insecurity. This need is guided by the need for survival in this world. Sexual intimacy is exciting and pleasurable initially, giving the persons involved the impression that it is heavenly. However, as one develops and moves towards spirituality and a higher way of life this intimacy loses its attraction. Being together also makes two persons share each other's status and feel stronger. Ultimately, the effect could wear off and even lead to conflict.

Intimacy based upon true love depends upon mutual acceptance and respect, care for each other's feelings, willingness to make adjustments even at the cost of personal inconvenience and gradually shaping oneself to create harmony with each other. This relationship involves tender caring and consideration for the other's needs, feelings and emotions. It also aims at getting to know each other better. This encourages one another to be drawn closer and develop an intimate relationship. Such is the kind of intimacy one develops within the home. Let us see how some of the popular relationships develop and can be nurtured for mutual benefit.

Marriage

Marriage is a formal union of a man and a woman by which they become husband and wife. It is socially recognised and legalizes sexual relations between the two, who go on to have children and raise a family. The institution of marriage exists in every culture. Every religion recommends its own rights and privileges for the couple. While marriage provides security, companionship, having and bringing up children, enjoying economic and social stability, it has its own problems. A marriage can be annulled through divorce.

The number of divorces is on the increase, causing hardship not only to the couple, but also to the children born of such wedlock. Most divorces are due to lack of commitment to the relationship. A selfish attitude and lack of willingness to share one's life with the partner have also led to broken marriages in almost every society around the world. Despite this, the institution of marriage has withstood the test of time and continues to be the foundation of a good civilized society.

Different cultures have adopted a variety of ways for a couple to get together and get married. In general, a man and a woman could be attracted to each other through interaction in a variety of situations, developing a bond that could lead to marriage. Such marriages are referred to as 'love' marriages. This has the approval of some cultures while others look down upon it. Marriages are arranged in some cultures, but again there are others who wonder how two persons unknown to each other could enjoy the intimacy that marriage involves. Both the systems have worked for some and failed for others.

Marriage involves a very complex relationship where a man and a woman get together to share their lives. They not only develop a sexual relationship that is the foundation of raising a family, but also develop emotional bonding. Since each of the partners is unique, comes from a different background, and one's feelings and emotions are involved in the relationship, the relationship is bound to be complex. Few appreciate that a man and a woman are built differently, driven by different hormones. In reality they are two individuals with separate hopes and aspirations. To live in harmony in marriage both need to follow a middle path, which involves mutual compromise of personal ideologies. This appears to be difficult, but couples who have attained this will confirm that marriage is a beautiful relationship leading both to happiness and fulfilment.

Every life is unique. So is every marriage. Yet mankind has put together observations and ideas on how one can enjoy happy married life. Here are a few observations worthy of consideration in one's life:

❖ No two marriages are alike. Nor are life situations. When people share experiences, one can interpret them in relation to past experiences.

❖ A happy marriage is no accident. It becomes possible through a deliberate effort by the husband and wife. It is a lifetime effort of two persons building a relationship through little acts of care and concern.

❖ Marriage is an equal relationship between a man and a woman. God intended man and woman to interact with each other as equals. Both are incomplete by themselves. Only when the two unite in marriage, they become complete. One complements the other. Both must contribute equally to the relationship.

❖ A successful marriage does not depend upon finding the right partner. Success comes from being the right partner.

❖ When a couple knows each other before marriage, it is referred to as a "love marriage". If they do not know each earlier, it is referred to as an "arranged marriage". Ideally, all "love marriages" should be successful. But they are not. One would expect most "arranged marriages" to fail. Many of them succeed. This makes it evident that a successful married relationship depends upon factors other than the couple knowing each other before marriage.

Think it over...

Marriage is popular because it combines the maximum of temptation with the maximum of opportunity.

— *G.B. Shaw*

- A marriage amongst cousins or near relations is accepted in some cultures. Many look down upon them. In the same way, most people are against marriages between couples of different castes, faiths, or religions. Marriages between close relatives are not advisable because of genetic abnormalities in the children. Inter-community marriages have their share of problems, but succeed when the partners are committed to the relationship.
- To evaluate the person one wants to marry, one should answer three questions. First, can we be good friends for a lifetime? Second, can he or she be a good father or mother to our children? And third, will I feel nice when I am seen in public with him or her? If the answer to the three questions is an emphatic "yes", one would have found a good partner.
- There is no such thing as a perfect marriage. The couple needs to work together to make it perfect.
- A major problem in most marriages is when one or both partners have very high expectations of each other. One must keep one's expectations from marriage within reasonable limits. Do not expect the partner to be a super human being. The hopes and aspirations of both the partners must be

fulfilled. This is possible only through equal give and take.

- Marriage involves adjustment not only between the couple, but also with the other partner's family. In some cultures, the two families also need to adjust with each other.
- To keep each other's families happy follow this simple rule: Do not praise your own family excessively. Do not criticize the spouse's family.
- Many persons get married to "imperfect" partners with the hope that they would change them after marriage. This is an erroneous thought. Old habits die hard. People resist change. Always remember that marriage is a relationship and not a compromise.
- Good marriages do not depend upon the man or the woman being more educated or economically superior. They depend upon how well the couple uses their skills and abilities to raise a good family and home together.
- In many families both the husband and the wife earn. In an ideal situation, both must have a clear understanding about financial matters. Some expenses could be met jointly, and yet both could control individual finances.
- With young men and women studying and working together and enjoying freedom, alliances build up and circumstances may compel the partners to be involved in physical relationships before marriage. It is not possible to suggest ways to handle these situations, each of which would be unique. It cannot be overlooked that these have a bad effect on

married life. One needs to be careful about such relationships.

- The courtship period between engagement and marriage is like a dream. It will pass off. One must keep one's feet on the ground.

- Sexual relationships between the couple play a significant role in every marriage. These cannot be ignored. The biological purpose of sex is to have children. However, human beings indulge in sexual relations as a part of physical intimacy. A positive attitude towards the relationship is necessary to make it satisfying for both the partners.

- When a child arrives, both the partners need to make adjustments. A child will need to be fed, clothed, kept clean, and be made happy and secure. This means personal involvement and financial implications. The personal attention of the wife will also be divided between the husband and the child. The husband could misunderstand this change.

- Quarrels are a part of married life. To love each other does not mean to give up one's individuality. There are bound to be some conflicts. Don't brothers and sisters quarrel? Since a certain amount of tension builds up when two persons live together, quarrels serve to provide a safety valve to this tension. They also serve to keep the partners alive to each other's needs. This results in better relations. Quarrels are not undesirable. The couple needs to develop a positive attitude towards them.

- Couples quarrel over irresponsible remarks about each other, about their families, about being loved, about sex, money, children, home and work. Quarrels erupt with a stray remark, particularly when one of the partners is not aware of the other partner's sensitivities.
- Conflicts in marriage should not be overlooked. They must be faced. When one sets out to resolve a conflict, it helps the partner to eliminate tension. It helps one to see reality. Conflicts also prepare people to be flexible and accept criticism as a part of life.
- When conflicts are difficult to handle, it is best that one partner withdraws saying, "I think I am upset. I cannot think straight. Let us talk about it later." Another way to handle a conflict is to say "sorry" and withdraw. An apology hurts the ego momentarily, but strengthens marital bonds. Good marriages are built upon giving and forgiving.
- Marriages succeed when one of the partners is unselfish. When both are unselfish the couple experiences bliss. Dada JP Vaswani explains, "Marriages fail when one of the partners refuses to under-stand". He explains the word 'understand' to mean the willingness to 'stand' a little 'under' (below) the other. This might hurt the ego, but strengthens the marriage.
- In an ideal situation, to every man, his wife should be the most important woman in the world. To every woman, her husband should be the most important man in the world.

- A woman feels loved when her husband cares for her through little acts of thoughtfulness. She desires to be appreciated sincerely for her charm, in being attractive to her husband and for enriching the life as a couple.
- Little acts of thoughtfulness by the husband and wife draw them closer to each other physically. This is the beginning of stronger emotional bonds.
- Love means different things to a man and to a woman. A man is easily aroused. To him love and sex is the same thing. His emotions are active, forceful, rise swiftly, and wane as rapidly. A woman is slow to arouse. To her sex means love. She likes to be loved and caressed. Her emotions are passive, receptive, and rise gently. She must be won over every time before both reach a common level of desire for each other.
- There can be no greater bliss than that of a happy married life. A man and a woman could be attracted to each other, but that is not love. Love grows only when the two share a concern for each other. Both must strive to keep the relationship alive. A happy married life is based upon this love.
- Marriage is not a relationship that can be taken for granted. It is a lifelong relationship. It must be lived day by day. It involves doing little things for each other. Sometimes one needs to be demanding. At other times one needs to compromise. All kinds of situations will come up. They will need to be handled with care. Values learnt in childhood act as a guiding force. Values become beliefs when one experiences life through intimate relationships.

Think it over...

A happy marriage is a new beginning of life, a new starting point for happiness and usefulness.

— *A.P. Stanley*

Staying Happily Married

To keep your married life happy and fulfilling, follow these simple rules:

- One must learn to respect, trust and support the spouse. This will reflect one's commitment to the relationship.
- Always count and remember your blessings. Look for what you have got from marriage and not what you had missed out.
- Love is not what most think it to be. Try to understand what it is. Give yourself to the relationship.
- Share common interests with your spouse. When a couple is focussed on common ideas, both work with greater zeal.
- Appreciate your spouse for what she or he is. Do not think of what she or he could be.
- The couple must always keep the communication channels open. The moment one of the partners goes into the silent mode, problems will surface.
- Never be shy to hold hands, embrace or kiss each other. Physical contact does great things to marriage.
- Go to bed together. Do remember that sexual relations are a natural part of a good marriage.

- One should never hesitate to apologise when things go wrong. An apology might hurt the ego, but will strengthen the relationship.

Strengthening Marriage

To strengthen marital relationship, here are ten things all married people should **avoid** :

- Criticize each other's families.
- Praise your own family only.
- Tell each other, "You don't love me."
- Tell each other, "You are not as smart or intelligent as I am."
- Tell each other that others find you more attractive.
- Tell each other that you could have found a better spouse.
- Doubt each other's intentions to look after the family.
- Attack each other's sense of fairness.
- Attack each other's sense of humour.
- Criticize each other's clothes.

Relationship With In-laws

A new relationship that emerges after marriage is that of in-laws. We cannot overlook that to both the partners their childhood families are important. Many significant experiences are attached with them. In cultures where family ties are strong both the husband and the wife would have strong bonds with the families. It is expected that like other things, each partner should accept the other's family with grace and offer them the same love and respect as one would give to one's own family. When this is done, the marital relationship becomes stronger.

One cannot overlook the many jokes that circulate all over the world about in-laws. Most of the jokes are in lighter vein just as we have jokes about doctors, lawyers, professors and several other professions. Having a little fun over this issue is obvious because one does not choose to develop a relationship with the in-laws. They come as a part of the package when a man and a woman tie the marital knot. In the interest of harmony, it becomes necessary to make a deliberate effort to build good relationships with them. Taking a positive attitude towards the issue, additional relationships should be a source of strength to anyone. Couples that build good relationships with each other's parents and relatives always stand to gain in many ways. In times of need, they always prove to be a great support.

In building good relationships with the in-laws always remember the simple rules of life. They are parents and relatives of your spouse. They need to be accepted and respected for whatever they are. Interaction with them may be limited, but it is necessary that the interaction is qualitative. Your spouse will forever be grateful for accepting those who are dear to him or her.

The Parents

Traditionally, there were joint families where everyone lived together in a large household. After marriage, the young woman would move to her husband's house. Everyone would enjoy a position in the family with the eldest as the head of the family. However, with the breakup of the joint family and people living as a nuclear family with the husband, wife and the children, the scenario has changed. The parents of the husband or the wife pay a visit occasionally. Sometimes it may be necessary for them to live with the family because of economic or health reasons. It is not unusual for a widowed father or mother to move in for similar reasons, besides the need for security.

The parents play a crucial role in bringing up and educating the children. Most of them do the best they are capable of. The Hindu scriptures tell us that the children are indebted to the parents for all the sacrifices they make in their upbringing, and this debt must be repaid by giving the parents respect throughout life and by caring for them when they grow old. This seems logical. However, it does not always happen that way. When children grow up and move out to raise their own families, their attention moves away from their parents, brothers and sisters and gets focussed on the spouse and the children. The interest in the parents unfortunately gets limited to how much more one can get from them in terms of property and money.

Few realize that if we stand tall today, it is because we started from where our parents left off, just as they started from where our grandparents left off. All progress has come about because each generation had something to contribute to building the family, the community and the nation. When we provide the very best to our children, it is with the hope that when we grow old our children would help us just as we are doing today. Our parents also thought likewise. If we forsake them today and leave them on their own without care, we should expect the same when our children grow up and we become too old to fend for ourselves. Parents continue to shower blessings on their children throughout life. We must seek them through love, care and concern.

Think it over ...

Happy are the families where the government of parents is the reign of affection, and obedience of the children the submission of love.

— *Bacon*

The Grandparents

As adults, very few people are fortunate to have grandparents. Most people experience the love and affection of grandparents only as children. More than the parents, it is the grandparents who indulge children. An important reason for this is that parents have far too many responsibilities to be indulging their children. On the other hand, the grandparents are free of those responsibilities and only have to enjoy with the grandchildren. Most adults who were fortunate to have experienced the love and care of grandparents when they were children will confirm that the time spent with them was quality time that engraved lifetime memories for them. Such is the love of grandparents.

Age and circumstances often wither a person and his or her spirit. Oblivious of the grandeur and importance the elderly people might have enjoyed in their younger years, most young people find the elderly quaint and demanding, so they try to avoid them. One cannot build or maintain relationships when one tries to avoid people, young or old. One should consider oneself fortunate to have grandparents. We should serve them rather than laugh at their limitations. If we observe them carefully, we would notice that their demands are few. More than anything else they seek dignity, particularly when they may be physically weak. They desire to be wanted. They would like to be recognised as a part of the society, not as have-beens. Are these needs too much to fulfil? Should these needs make them the butt of a joke or a laughing matter?

The person who wants to build good relationships should accept people as they are, whether they are children, young adults, elderly or the aged. These are different phases of life and must be accepted wholeheartedly.

Children

Everyone professes to love children. One would expect relationships with children to be good. However, the worldwide observations do not confirm this assertion. In most developed countries, the population growth figures are static, or even negative. This makes it evident that with greater comfort that accompanies development, people are losing interest in having children. Another significant observation is that as soon as the children are old enough to earn they drift away from the parents, making it evident that economic considerations are stronger than the parent-child relationship.

In less developed parts of the world one observes a marked growth in the population figures. Although infant mortality is high in some of these areas, yet the population figures are growing. This is attributed to lack of education and knowledge of contraception. While instinctively parents assert their love for children, they are unable to look after them. Many children are compelled to work rather than go to school. The girl child suffers more. In underdeveloped and developing nations, we frequently hear of child labour. Economic compulsions overtake instinctive love.

In some cultures people are obsessed with having a boy, who can be the heir. They pay greater emphasis on the upbringing and education of the male child.

Midway between the two situations we come across people who want to raise a family with two children, preferably a boy and a girl. With better economic conditions, parents are able to spend more on the children, providing them more amenities, better schools and comforts. But with both the father and the mother working to increase the family income, there is a marked degradation of family values. The parents are spending very little quality time with the children. They are compensating this with increased indulgent activities. Although the children enjoy this, they complain about the lack of quality time spent with them. This creates a gap between the two generations. Both the parents and the children suffer from the outcome of such a relationship. While the parents are too busy earning money and securing a high position in the society, the children feel unwanted and might gradually drift away. Generally, this is the parent-child relationship one gets to see in the modern day society.

Every child is unique. He is an adult in the making. As an adult he will be like others in that he will be unique, right from his point of view to being sensitive to various things just like other people. It is true that parents work hard to provide education and comfort to the child, and have certain dreams for him or her, but the child should not be forced to fulfil their parent's dream without a second thought. The purpose of education is to make a person capable of making a place for oneself in the world. Once a child's education is over, the parents need to accept him or her as an adult in his or her own right. It is for the person to put his or her education to the best use. Parents do not need to keep showing direction to their children all the time.

Here are some observations on relationships with children as they grow up from infancy to adulthood:

- Both the mother and the father should be responsible for the care and upbringing of children. While the mother's role is important, the father's role is also important in providing good values.
- Children who are breastfed are not only healthy, but also grow up to be more secure adults.
- Generally, parents try to relive their childhood through their children. They try to shape them as they deem fit. However, they are shocked when the children turn out to be different kinds of adults.
- All children need to be well nourished, kept clean, warm and secure. What they need more is a rich storehouse of memories from which they can draw in adult life. This can be provided only through little acts of care and concern by the parents.
- Daughters have a strong attachment with the fathers, and childhood experiences influence the selection of a husband and how married life can be lived. Sons are more attached to the mother, but identify themselves with the father.
- The greatest gift parents can give their child is a happy childhood. This happiness does not depend upon how much the parents pamper the child, or the amount of money they spend, but on the

pleasant memories they can give. These come from patience, love and understanding the parents share with the child and also the quality time they are willing to spend with the child.

- ❖ The foundations of all adult habits are laid in childhood. Since the child does what the parents guide him to do, the parents need to be careful.
- ❖ All children are very observant and attach great significance to their parents' action. It is in these early years that a child learns to accept or reject the principles of truth, honesty and selflessness.
- ❖ Self-confidence is an important characteristic in all adults. The foundation is laid in childhood through positive encouragement by the parents. Parents must help their children to develop wide interests and lasting friendships.
- ❖ Good money values are also learnt in childhood. Parents must provide the opportunities for children to learn what is money and how it should be used.
- ❖ As the children grow up, it is the parents' responsibility to teach a child how to cope with the physical and emotional changes during adolescence. They must also teach them about sex so that they do not get wrong information from dubious sources.
- ❖ Above all else the parents need to train the child to live independently as an adult by learning to cope with all kinds of people and situations.

Parents provide best education, training and care to the child. Even if a child moves away as an adult, the parent-child relationship should not be affected. Good relationships last a lifetime.

Think it over...

The most important thing a father can do for his children is to love their mother.

— *Theodore Hesburgh*

Other Relatives

One does not need to interact too often with relatives because they may live away, but in joint families where uncles, aunts and cousins live together, it is natural to build up relationships according to personal affinity with each other. These relationships are like others. No fixed rules can be made to make them congenial and worthwhile. One needs to make an effort to develop a good relationship. If one wants to live in harmony with everyone, one should be prepared to sacrifice one's convenience to take care and serve others. One may not be rewarded for these efforts immediately. God is watching. Harmonious relationships are always rewarding. One is never alone in times of need.

Think it over...

Self-preservation is the first law of nature; self-sacrifice the highest rule of grace.

— *Anon*

Domestic Help

It is often said that a good spouse, a good friend and a good servant are all gifts of God. Ask anyone who is so blessed. He will confirm it repeatedly. On the contrary, some people always look down upon domestic help as poor and needy people. Yes, they may be needy. To them it is a necessity to work and support their family. But it should not belittle a person because he or she is offering their labour in return for the salary they get. They might be poor, but they are human beings who deserve to be treated with dignity. People who understand this simple truth are always fortunate to enjoy good relationships with the domestic staff, ensuring happiness for themselves and for those who support them in building a happy home.

Think it over...

Expect not more from servants than is just; reward them well if they observe their trust; nor with them pride or cruelty invade, since God and nature them our brothers made.

— *Denham*

Points to Ponder...

- A man and a woman develop intimacy and raise a family in the precincts of a home.
- Good relationships do not just happen. They need to be created through love, care and understanding.
- Relationships within the home are marked with physical and emotional intimacy.
- The institution of marriage exists in every culture and religion around the world.
- Marriage is a complex relationship where both the husband and the wife need to persevere to keep it alive and fulfilling.
- The couple must be united in order to face the pressures of married life.

- A family is much larger than just the couple and their children.
- When one respects the elders in the family, one can expect a similar treatment when their children grow up.
- Children learn all major values early in life within the home.
- Love always begets love from others.

Relationships At The Workplace

Everyone spends the whole day at the workplace. With greater competition in every sphere of life, the office hours are getting longer, working pressures stiffer and the working trends rapidly changing. However, the old adage, "Business is People," continues to hold good at the workplace.

Every day one meets many people. Besides the colleagues at the workplace, there will be the subordinates, the senior management and a whole lot of other people who may visit as suppliers, contractors, consultants or customers. It becomes necessary to leave a good impression upon them for promoting the aims of the organization one is working for. This is by no means a small order. People come in all shapes and sizes and have great expectations. Keeping them happy and satisfied is not a day's job. One needs to do it day after day, week after week, throughout the year, and still more. One needs to be well equipped for it.

To make it easy to deal with a large variety of people, one needs to develop good relationships at the workplace.

We have earlier discussed the basics of building and maintaining good relationships. We have also discussed how one needs to maintain relationships at home. Let us now consider some of the special aspects of dealing with the people one works with or comes in contact at the workplace.

People at the Workplace

A person's success is greatly influenced by the way one gets along with people at the workplace. Irrespective of what one does for a living, one will need to deal with people. There will be customers, clients and suppliers. The most important are those we work with. Many may be working as subordinates. Some as colleagues. Others would be in higher positions. With almost one-fourth of life spent at the workplace, much of it in dealing with people, one cannot ignore the influence these relationships have on one's life. To succeed one needs to understand relationships at the workplace in more detail.

Working with Subordinates

A subordinate would obviously hold a lower position, and may also enjoy lesser income and benefits. However, that does not make him or her inferior to you. Provided the person has average intelligence and is given encouragement and guidance, he or she may be capable to rise to your position or even higher. Subordinates are human beings. They have a home and a family to support. Their needs are important to them. They deserve to be treated with respect, just as one would treat a member of a team. Irrespective of one's position at the workplace, everyone seeks respect. When this respect is denied to them, the self-esteem suffers and the person denying this need is looked at with contempt.

Everyone desires to rise in life. Promotions depend upon the recommendations of the immediate boss. To gain recognition many suggestions to enhance quality and productivity will be offered. These aim at seeking approval and appreciation. The ideas offered might be useless. They might have already been tried earlier. However, suggestions should never be turned down without a fair hearing. One must be patient. If a suggestion is not useful, explain why. This way the initiative of the person who might have worked hard to bring it will not be dampened. When new ideas are appreciated and useful ones accepted, people strive hard to promote productivity and profitability.

A person's success depends upon the people one works with. To promote productivity, they must be aware what is expected of them. They must also know how they will benefit by becoming more productive. A person works more zealously for personal benefit than when the benefit goes to others.

Workers must be well motivated. They must look up to you as their leader and not as one who only passes orders. When dealing with subordinate staff at different levels, one should deal with them through those who coordinate their work. The working environment for the staff must be congenial. Suggest how work can be interesting and also how monotony and fatigue can be avoided.

Always express confidence in the workers. A part of the responsibility can be delegated to them. Let them make the minor decisions. This gives a sense of involvement besides reducing the pressure of your work. This also gives one an opportunity to gauge their ability about handling additional responsibilities. Encouragement, appreciation and praise motivate the workers. If things go astray, do not hesitate to share part of the blame for their actions. It is human to make mistakes. Accept them as part of work. When you know that the mistake could have been avoided, explain it to the workers. This way you will always enjoy their confidence.

Lack of self-control compels many to become angry and threaten an erratic worker. Do not let this happen. Rarely can these threats be carried out. A loss is likely to upset a person emotionally. In such a state one does not realize that threats are not practical. Similarly, do not promise what you cannot deliver. To swallow one's threats and promises can be a very humiliating experience. This is a sure way to lose the confidence of a good worker.

A person in position is expected to be fair. One must be fair about distribution of work, discipline at the workplace and promotions. Workers can be resentful about these matters. One needs to be fair in handling complaints and breakdown of discipline. Be understanding, but firm. Take firm decisions. Be specific. Do not let anyone feel that you have varying standards for dealing with different workers. Let everyone enjoy your confidence and place his or her faith in you. Do not demand respect. You must win it through your work.

Working with Colleagues

Working with colleagues should not be difficult. Everyone is likely to have separate responsibilities. One would only need to be cordial, friendly and helpful. One should share mutual interests and ensure that there is harmony amongst everyone. When the activities are inter-linked and the productivity of one affects the others, one will have to be careful not to let down the teamwork. An inefficient member of the team makes the chain weak. To carry the person along one will need to use tact and patience. Fretting and fuming cannot improve matters. It would be better to analyse the problems, talk about them, suggest solutions and help implement them. The senior management should be made aware of the situation. If things do not improve, it may become necessary to refer the matter to them.

Colleagues do not appreciate when one of them tries to act superior in ability or intelligence. One could be better. Everyone may know about it. Yet nobody likes to accept the fact that others are superior. Rather than being helpful, people pull the person down in weaker moments. Everyone must contribute the best to the team. The senior management is always on the lookout to spot capable workers. When they see one, they will move the person a step ahead of others. When promoted, one should not boast about one's ability. The colleagues think no less of their own abilities. You could tell them that luck has favoured you more than them.

The Senior Management

A person's growth at the workplace depends on how the immediate boss or the senior management looks at the abilities and performance of the individual. This makes it necessary to keep the senior management satisfied. Some seek promotions through the back door. They make this possible by flattering the persons concerned, or by doing them out-of-the-way favours. Such methods appeal only to an unscrupulous few. At the workplace, productivity and profits are important considerations. No activity in the workplace can be justified without them.

In a well-managed organization, the senior colleagues are good role models. There is much that one can learn from them. It should be a pleasure to work with them. The ability to handle responsibility and work well is important to every boss. To grow at the workplace one must know what is expected. The top management is always focussed on increasing production and profits. They are aware that in any activity there will be problems, shortcomings and even failures. They expect that a responsible person should be able to recognize the cause for such failings and find reasonable solutions. Mistakes should provide opportunities to learn. Each mistake should pave the way to flawless working.

The top management understands human problems well. They know how to win the confidence of the workers quickly. However, occasionally one may have to work with a difficult person. The person may be an expert in a specialized subject, but may lack understanding of human nature. Despite the hardship it may cause, one must deal amiably with such persons. His lack of understanding should not discourage you. Harsh criticism should not be responded with bitterness. One must try to understand what he desires and why he desires it. If you have failed to perform well, analyze the situation and tell him about it. Tact and patience are useful tools under such circumstances.

When the management appreciates the work, do not take the entire credit for the success. Share it with the entire staff. You will be rewarded for your modesty. Praise your efforts conservatively. When there is a problem or failure, step forward to take responsibility for it. Ensure that it does not repeat itself. Nobody likes a person who professes to be perfect and blames others for shortcomings. Act reasonably. You will be accepted for what you are.

A person's desire to learn and perform better is always appreciated. When a person does a little more than what is expected, one immediately understands that the person is capable of more responsibility. The ability to analyze past failures and to profit by the knowledge is another quality which is immediately recognized and takes one to higher positions in life.

The Ideal Boss

Every person has a secret desire of working for an ideal employer and boss. In a job, one seeks maximum benefits and security of service. However, it does not happen that way. One can only seek mutual benefit where both the employer and the employee find satisfaction.

Employers are generally categorized according to what they offer by way of working conditions, pay scales, security of service, fringe benefits, bonus, etc. In any job we cannot ignore the human factor and the existence of a good employer-employee relationship which helps differentiate good and bad employers. In an ideal relationship, an employee is treated as an individual entity and not as another machine or piece of equipment.

Government jobs offer the maximum security of service. The entry into these jobs is through competitive examinations. Basic qualifications and merit are very important. The larger companies offer better pay scales and benefits to their employees as compared to the smaller ones. However, they offer limited opportunities of gaining experience and growth. In a smaller concern, a young person is entrusted with greater responsibility. He gets a good on-the-job experience that gives him the confidence to handle responsibility independently. This is a very important qualification when the right opening shows up. Good relationships with the boss must always be based upon ability and performance.

Etiquette in the Office

One is generally at one's best at the workplace. Every workplace has a definite purpose. To achieve it discipline is important. Some rules are written. Many are not. Those which are not written come within the working style or customs adopted by the organization. These become a part of office etiquette.

One-third of one's working life is spent at the workplace. The way one behaves is as important as the work he or she does. The behaviour is reflected in the image one projects. Good etiquette and manners contribute to make an office a congenial place to work. One can follow these simple guidelines:

- Every office adopts a dress code. One must be dressed appropriately.

- Every office has a working culture pertaining to handling of documents, files, office equipment and stationery. Every evening the table must be clear, the documents should have been filed and the files put in the cabinets.
- The time for midday tea or coffee should not be an occasion for a little chat.
- The toilets at the workplace must be so used as to leave them in a condition that you would like to find them.
- All kinds of people visit the workplace. One must observe self-restraint and patience in dealing with them. Tact and patience are useful tools.
- The telephones at the workplace are often misused. One must ensure its proper use.
- Do not misuse office time. You are being paid for it. When time is used for any other purpose than work, you are stealing time.
- Avoid misuse of office equipment like calculators, typewriters, fax machines, computers, printers and photostat machines. Office furniture is another item of abuse. Avoid this misuse.
- Office vehicles are for limited use. Use them within limits you are entitled to. Similarly, entertainment allowances are strictly for professional use.
- When men and women work in the same office, there must be courtesy and decency. Personal and professional activities must not be mixed. Treat each other as a member of a team.
- Every office has a definite policy regarding additional working time. If lady employees need to

stay late, they must be provided transport to return to their homes.

Think it over...

Five things are requisite to a good officer – ability, clean hands, dispatch, patience, and impartiality.

— *Penn*

Working as a Team

With every kind of work becoming very competitive, it is not possible for a person to give his or her best alone. It has been observed that people working as a team are better able to enhance productivity and profitability at the workplace than when they handle responsibility individually. A team could be of two or more members. While one would act as leader and coordinator of the team, the others would pool in their skills and abilities to attain the goal.

We have earlier observed that every person is different and unique with personal sensitivities. This makes the work of the team leader difficult. One will need to know and understand the skills, abilities, strengths and weaknesses of each team member. The team leader should also know how he or she will respond in a given set of circumstances. Since each member of the team would respond differently, one needs special skills to handle a team.

To get the best from teamwork, it is necessary to inspire confidence and enthusiasm in the team. Every member of the team must be well acquainted with the purpose of the task in hand. This would require good communication skills in the leader and the team. In some circumstances written skills are important, but in majority of cases one requires good speaking skills. The body language is equally important. It reflects the level of confidence of the team. The team must be convinced that the leader is sincere and committed.

Management gurus repeatedly tell us that teams perform better than individuals working separately. People ask why this should be so? How can the performance of a team be better than the performance of the members of the team? Who contributes towards the additional performance? This fact is explained by Napoleon Hill in his famous work *The Law of Success*. He calls the phenomenon 'The Law of the Mastermind'. According to him when two or more persons get together to attain a common goal, both are endowed with more power than each could wield individually. We see the practical application of this law in everyday life.

Have you ever observed a young man and a woman who get together in marriage? Soon after marriage they become more responsible and focused in life? Have you observed that a partnership firm functions better than a proprietorship business? In the same way, can you understand why companies grow when a well-focused Board of Directors leads them? Organizations grow and develop when a good team leads them.

The success of the team depends upon the harmony the leader has been able to develop within the team. This requires an understanding of human nature. This comes slowly through greater knowledge and experience. The emphasis must be on attaining a common goal and not on developing complete harmony amongst the team members. This is neither desirable nor possible.

Sharing Goals

A team cannot succeed without definite goals. Setting goals is to know one's destination. One who does not know the destination is only moving. When you do not know where you are going, you reach there – nowhere!

To be useful a goal must be:

- **Specific and measurable**. If it is not, it cannot be a goal.
- **Challenging**. If it were not challenging, it would not be worthwhile.
- **Achievable**. If it cannot be achieved in particular circumstances, it can be counter productive.
- **Time-bound**. If it were not time-bound, one would never be motivated to achieve it.
- **Shared**. If it were not shared with those who are concerned with it, it would be difficult to attain it.

The goal must be written down and shared by the team. The sharing process must begin when a project or activity is conceived and the team to attain it is agreed upon. When every member of the team is involved with the details of the goal, each person feels more responsible towards attaining it. This way the chances of a member letting down the team are eliminated.

It may be necessary to set a variety of goals. There would be long-term goals and short-term goals. Depending upon the activity there will be the need for annual goals, quarterly goals, monthly goals and also weekly goals. These would ensure success at every step. Sometimes it is necessary to adopt product goals to ensure quality at every step. There would also be operational goals for proper utilization of the workers' skills. Consumer goals ensure happy consumers through better products and services. Besides these there are secondary goals that arise from current operations. All these goals are necessarily shared goals. To attain them everyone in the team must be involved. This promotes good relationships amongst the team members.

Delegating Responsibility

Just as responsibility is shared amongst the team members, delegating responsibility helps improve one's productivity. When the lesser important work is delegated to subordinates, one gets more time to plan for the future and do other important things needing superior skills. Everyone knows that it can be done, but most people avoid it for a common fear that the subordinate might not perform as well as one would like to. By lack of trust in the people at the workplace one sends out wrong signals.

A common cause for not delegating work is the fear that the person may soon become a competitor for one's position. The person may displace one who delegated the responsibility. This may happen if the person delegates work and personally does nothing. When a part of the work is delegated to a person of lesser skills and ability and one would personally do what needs superior skills that come from greater experience, there would be nothing to fear. This way new people are trained to handle that particular activity. The person rises to the next higher position, making place for one who deserves it.

The fear that the person may not be able to meet deadlines is another reason why people avoid delegation of responsibilities. Nobody wants to be let down at the last minute. This would happen only if the work is delegated and not followed up. That would defeat the very purpose of delegation.

If one desires to grow at the workplace, one needs to learn the art of effective delegation. The secret of being effective is not in doing everything well oneself. One needs to choose the right people to do the right jobs, leading them to success.

How does one ensure effective delegation? Where does one find the right people? How can one maintain good relationships at the workplace? Everyone searches answers to these questions. Before one can effectively delegate responsibility to others, one must be able to perform that particular task or must know how it can be performed. One should never consider any work too small or belittling to do personally. Such an attitude sends out negative messages to the person who is assigned to do the work. This would invite failure even before one has begun.

Here are some observations about delegating responsibility:

- Delegation involves passing some of one's work and authority to others while one still continues to be accountable for the results.
- Delegation always involves a certain amount of risk. One can keep this risk within safe limits by keeping an eye on the assignment.

- Identify what needs to be done, and what is the time frame. Can the task be broken up into smaller activities, together contributing to attain a goal? What are these activities? What are the risks involved in delegating these activities to other colleagues?
- Evaluate the abilities of the people who can support you. Are you aware of their skills and abilities? Can you match some of these skills and abilities to the activities you have identified? Can the persons fulfil these within the available time frame?
- Discuss what needs to be done with the person you consider worthy of the responsibility. Does the person know what is the ultimate goal? Is the person aware how his or her contribution is going to affect the goal? Does the person know that periodic evaluation and reporting are part of the responsibility?
- Keep a check on how the members of the team are performing. Is everyone reporting the progress? Is the progress satisfactory? Will it be possible to finish the task within the time frame? If there were any problems, have they been suitably addressed? The answers will lead one to success.
- When things go wrong, do not panic. One must remain cool, particularly when a crisis is brewing. Call a meeting of the team. Assess the problem realistically. Jointly agree on remedial measures. Re-assign responsibilities if necessary.
- Congratulate the team for success. In the end convey your gratitude to every member of the team for his or her contribution in attaining the goal

successfully. This will ensure better performance the next time.

Think it over...

They that govern make least noise, as they that row the barge do work and puff and sweat, while he that governs sits quietly at the stern, and scarce is seen to stir.

— *Selden*

Plan of Action

Once goals are set the next obvious step is to plan how to achieve them. A good plan of action is the ideal way to achieve what one has set out to do. In an ideal situation, the team members should also be involved in the planning process. One needs to be careful because some team members could be more aggressive than others and may dominate the planning activities. To ensure that everyone gets a fair share in the planning process, one would need to offer equal opportunity to everyone, making sure that nobody dominates. This is a tricky situation, but in the interest of success one must be careful about it.

The plan of action would need to have two components– the macro plan that sets overall goals, and the micro plans that define short-term or day-to-day goals and activities. The team members must share responsibilities at this stage. One must ensure that everyone's skills and abilities are used for the benefit of the project in hand. Once again, some of the team members may seek easier work or work that would highlight their contribution rather than ensure the overall success of the project. The leader would need to intervene and hand out responsibilities to ensure the best results. The leader must not only be fair but also appear to be so.

It would be appropriate for every member of the team to be aware of the priorities of different components of the project in hand. It is not enough just to complete one's share of work within the time frame. It is equally important that the priorities must first be defined and thereafter be followed to ensure that no member of the team feels let down or any aspect of the project suffers. When the team members are aware of the priorities of the goals, success will be ensured.

Motivating the Team

Motivation aims at touching the emotions and feelings of people. If a person can touch a person's emotions, there is immediate motivation. This comes from the promise of fulfilment of a need. One must always use positive ways to motivate team members. One could arouse greed through negative motivation. By encouraging greed people indulge in malpractices. One can arouse a mob to shout and destroy through a negative suggestion that touches the emotions. Even good people are known to behave irrationally in a mob. It takes sometime before the negative influence wears off.

The most popular way to motivate people at the workplace is through money. Attractive pay packages including perks like a house, a car, and amenities like free healthcare and an annual holiday package for the family are popular forms of motivation. In everyday practice it is common to see business houses offering a variety of incentives to consumers, retail and wholesale stores and their own personnel.

How can the workforce be motivated to achieve desired goals? Here are a few simple suggestions:

- Establish harmony within the workforce. They must be in agreement about established goals and procedures.
- Everyone must be aware of the purpose of the goal. They must know why it has to be attained.
- Everyone must be aware of each other's responsibilities. Without it there would be confusion.
- Everyone must be aware of the time frame. Time is money. It must always be respected at the workplace.
- Make everyone accountable for his or her responsibility. One must report progress regularly. Without reporting one can easily slip or fail.
- Look out for unexpected obstacles and problems. There could be some miscalculation of facts, figures and time.
- Have backup arrangements in place. There can be emergencies.
- Always appreciate and reward good work. You will get better response the next time.
- In the event of a failure to attain one's goal, do not blame any one person for the failure. Share the blame with others.

- Analyse the efforts that were made. You must search for the cause of failure.
- Learn from your failure. It is not wrong to fail. It is wrong not to learn from failure. Treat failure as a temporary defeat. This attitude will ensure an early success.

Think it over...

The two great movers of the human mind are the desire of good, and the fear of evil.

— *Johnson*

Office Romances

With both men and women working together and having lot of things in common, it is not unusual for affairs to develop at the workplace. One usually looks at it with the boss having an affair with his pretty secretary. However, it is no longer limited to that. A middle-aged lady boss could be having an affair with an assistant; two unmarried workers could be dating each other before getting married. It could also be two married persons having an affair for the fun of it, without any interest in breaking their existing marriages for they may have children.

Besides the two individuals involved in an affair, an affair at the workplace involves the employer also because the affair takes place during office time. Some employers do not care about it. Their attitude is clear, "As long as my work does not suffer, why should I interfere with my workers' personal lives?" Others look at it differently, "If one of them is taking advantage of his or her position and favouring the partner at my cost, why should I take it quietly?"

Legal issues pertaining to affairs at the workplace also need consideration. Some organizations do not hire married couples. If they do, they place them in different areas of work. Other organisations look down upon affairs in the office. As a part of the employment agreement, they have a clause that makes it mandatory for a person to bring an affair to the notice of the management. From the management's point of view, this is important because at some stage an issue of sexual harassment could be raised, affecting the reputation of the organization. Some organizations also include clauses that if the single employee marries another employee in the organization, then one of the partners would have to immediately resign. If they do not inform the management, the services of both the employees could be terminated as a punishment.

While more men and women are working together at the workplace, the variety of affairs and situations are becoming complex. The management is concerned about such situation as it affects its reputation. A person who desires to have good relationships at the workplace needs to be especially careful about office affairs and how the management looks upon them.

Think it over...

Every young man would do well to remember that a successful business stands on the foundation of morality.

— *H.W. Beecher*

Changing Values at the Workplace

With women becoming economically independent, their dependence upon their husbands and their attitudes are undergoing a vast change. Men and women who work from morning till late evening are too tired to find fulfilment with their wife or husband, who may be equally tired. They may seek such fulfilment at the workplace, thereby living a dual life. One may question the morality of such a situation, but it is all in the attitude. Freedom is expressed in a variety of forms.

Earlier, bosses were looked down upon for seeking favours of the secretary, but today people argue that when people persistently work hard and go out to seek favours to rise in life, what is the harm if the employee indulges in these relationships to seek promotions and rise higher in the organization and in life? The bosses too justify it by saying that it is all part of work. The truth is that people are willing to give in to their instincts rather than observe self-control.

Many wonder why these things happen in the office. It would be understandable for the unmarried to get involved, but why the married lot? For one thing, everyone is at his or her best in the office. One is dressed appropriately, one is trained to smile and speak well as part of the responsibilities in the office. So there is a marked contrast from what the spouse appears at home. With all defenses down, one is bound to look ordinary. Yet another cause for these affairs is personal insecurity at the workplace. By pairing up, one seeks support and courage from the other. Finding fulfilment is another reason for experimenting with these relationships.

All these things appear all right until such time that everyone concerned accepts this intimacy. When expectations emerge from these relationships, which they always will because it is a part of human nature, these relationships become burdensome. They begin to affect existing relationships also. One may lose the confidence and respect of one's spouse, the children and the family.

The right person and place to find emotional and sexual fulfilment is not a partner at the workplace, but a spouse at home. The family continues to be the basic institution upon which the society is built. The husband-wife relationship withstands the test of time. All religions commend it. A person needs to understand the relationship well. A happy married life opens way to congenial relationships at the workplace.

Sexual Harassment

With men and women working together, a problem that many organizations are concerned about is that of sexual harassment at the workplace. There have been instances where large corporations have come under severe criticism when instances of sexual harassment came to surface and were blown out of proportion by the media. Business organizations are giving special attention to ensure freedom from such problems.

While many organizations assert that the problem is more imaginary than real, but figures collected during surveys tell another story. In the United States, it is estimated that 40 to 60% women workers are sexually harassed. European figures place it at 40 to 50%. Women do not make sexual harassment claims alone. Men too have made claims of harassment by female bosses. The number of complaints made by men being harassed may be lesser than those for women, but it is estimated that of all cases reported, one-third are men and two-third are women.

Sexual harassment is an unwelcome attention of sexual nature and by its very nature it is a complex problem involving two persons with different intentions and perceptions. Since it affects the reputation of the organization and also the relationships the workers enjoy as a part of their responsibilities, it is important that one must be aware of the existence of this problem and steer away from it as far as possible.

Points to Ponder...

- Good relationships at the workplace lead one to success.
- Subordinate staff is as human as others. Always treat them with respect.
- Always work with colleagues as one of them.
- Senior colleagues are good role models.
- Good relationships with the boss must be based upon ability and performance.
- No workplace can be effective without office etiquette.
- Working as a team is more effective than working independently.
- Sharing goals and responsibilities with the team makes it effective.
- Everyone looks up to a person who motivates him or her to succeed.
- The workplace is no place for romances and affairs.
- Moral values are fast changing at the workplace.
- All managements look at sexual harassment at the workplace as an issue of great concern.

Relationships in the Society

The ability to get along well with people is one of the most valuable abilities a person can possess. Those who occupy high positions successfully establish good relations with people not only because of their business and professional skills, but also because they are comfortable with all kinds of people. Besides the people at home and the workplace one needs to deal with a variety of people. Other than friends and acquaintances, there is the liftman, the building guards, the gardener and the domestic help. In the marketplace there are shopkeepers, salesmen and shop assistants. Even the milkman, the laundryman and the postman, who visit our home every day, develop a relationship that cannot be easily defined, but it exists all the same. Even the people on the street place certain responsibilities upon us.

Success in business and professional life is visible through our lifestyle. This cannot be possible without the relationships one develops with people who indirectly contribute towards it. The superstructure of success is built upon the foundation of good relationships. People seek harmony wherever they go. They gravitate towards people with similar temperament. The knowledge of good human relations comes from keen observation and understanding of human behaviour. This knowledge cannot be passed on entirely to even the most dear ones. Everyone must experience it personally. Since it involves dealing with people coming from different backgrounds, it continues to challenge everyone who desires to maintain good relationships.

People and Happiness

People are not the same to everyone. They are fun to those who find happiness with them. One enjoys their company at home, workplace or in society. The secret does not lie in going overboard with pleasing people. Nobody has ever succeeded in pleasing everyone. It is just not possible. One should not sacrifice personal happiness to make others happy. One needs to live a balanced life that has a place for everyone.

It is easy to share one's time with friends and companions. Others also need attention and kindness. One's efforts are rewarded through better service and happiness wherever one goes. The relationships may not be deep, but they can be worthwhile. One can enjoy the relationship yet stay aloof. One's relationship with people must be congenial and satisfying.

The people one comes across in everyday life are as important as those at the workplace. Their opinions affect a person's position in society. To achieve harmony and goodwill, one should offer them the usual courtesies. Every person is an individual in his or her own right. Patience and an understanding heart are assets when dealing with people. The lift attendant, the building guards, the gardener and our own domestic help deserve our attention. We cannot ignore taxi drivers, shop attendants, salesmen, and the staff at clubs, restaurants and hotels that we visit. When one radiates enthusiasm and goodwill, one gets better service. One should never look down upon those who serve us. Thank them for the service they render. Expression of gratitude helps build goodwill. Accept special favours graciously. It is immaterial how small the service is. An attitude of gratitude is always appreciated. It comes back as still better service.

Understanding People

We should look at people from their point of view. Everyone considers himself or herself to be the most important person in the world. His or her name is the sweetest word that they like to hear. One wants to be accepted and treated as a unique person. Personal emotions and feelings are very important. These must be respected and honoured. Everyone desires to have a healthy body, a secured home, a happy family, a secured livelihood, and a feeling of personal fulfilment. One likes to feel important and seeks appreciation for the good work he or she does. To every individual, his or her personal problems are unique and nobody could face them better. Everyone has a personal philosophy about life which he or she insists is the best and would like to live by it. On analysis one cannot help but agree and accept the individual and the reality.

Unfortunately, only one out of every twenty people looks at life from a positive viewpoint. Negative thoughts and feelings predominate the lives of the other nineteen. The lives of the vast majority are ruled by fears and phobias of all kinds. Most people who indulge in these fears are unaware that they are imaginary, a creation of their own mind. When reminded, people will emphatically disagree that they failed because they are negatively oriented. They will rationalize their actions, blaming the failures on other people and situations. Unwilling to change, they continue to live like slaves of invisible monsters. As they have not known a life which is free from unnecessary worries, they do not know what they are missing.

Winning People Over

To win people over, it is necessary to make them feel wanted. Accept them as they are. Accept what is dear to them. Appreciate them sincerely. Remember their names. Inquire about their home and family. Make them feel secure. Appreciate whatever they do for the society. Take interest in them. Listen to what they wish to say. Respect their hopes and aspirations. This gives them confidence and self-esteem. People seek listeners more than they seek advice. Lend a sympathetic ear. Speak sparingly but well. To be one of them, speak in their language. People are generally interested in many things. To be one of them, speak their language and share similar interests. A person with a wide range of interests finds it easy to get along with others.

Be enthusiastic. Share your optimism with others. It is contagious. It spreads quickly. When one takes interest in others' welfare, they are attracted towards you. Extend the usual courtesies like saying "thank you", "excuse me", "I beg your pardon" or "I'm sorry" in everyday life. Accept good time management as a part of daily life. Respect people's time. Compliment others for their achievements. Personal success is important to everyone. Praise and appreciation help win over people. Avoid gossip and criticism. It has never done anybody any good. Avoid getting into an argument. You may win the argument but will lose a friend. Do not be concerned with others more than is necessary. Do not give advice unless it is asked for. Even when you know that your suggestions are true and factual, leave the option of accepting it to the person seeking it. When defamatory facts about others come to your knowledge, bury them rather than repeat them. Never speak or act in a manner that your honour or integrity would be doubted. When people seek your help, do not spill out your own problems. People seek help from those who are self-sufficient, not from those who are in trouble. When you smile, people smile back at you. Laugh and people will laugh with you.

Ethics and People

Shortcuts to winning people are not worthwhile even though they produce quick results. Flattery is a common tool used to win people over. Many throw lavish parties and shower presents to attract the gullible few. They appear to achieve immediate success. However, relationships built upon such activities do not last long. They are based on material benefits and not on emotional bonds which should form the basis of all lasting relationships.

There is no substitute for sincerity, integrity and honourable conduct to win people over for a long-term relationship. One with a noble character, who is known for truthfulness and honesty, is accepted as a responsible citizen, as one worthy of everyone's confidence. A virtuous life does not produce immediate results. One is acknowledged and recognized only over a period of time. One builds goodwill in society by being thoughtful towards others. Kindness, sympathy and understanding, together with love, add to the strength of one's character. Goodwill that emerges is a joy forever. When one enjoys the goodwill of people, one can be proud to possess the finest form of power that anyone can wield. When this power is used to benefit others, it grows. When used for self-appeasement, it diminishes. Self-sufficiency is a great power-builder. All people look up to those who are so blessed.

Greeting People

It is customary to greet people. A greeting helps break the communication barrier. Some greet by saying, "Good morning" or "Hello", others may say "*Namaste*" or "*Namaskar*". Others prefer saying, "*Ram Ramji*" or "*Jai Hari Krishna*". Sikhs greet by saying, "*Sat Shri Akal*". Muslims say, "*Aadabarz*". Whatever be the form of greeting, it immediately removes barriers between people. It creates a feeling of oneness amongst them. Some prefer to shake hands. Others join hands to say, "*Namaskar*." Some wave to say "Hi!" Some embrace. A few kiss on the cheek. Greeting each other brings people closer. Greetings express thoughtfulness for the other person. They make it easier for people to get them talking. Greetings motivate and inspire people to develop friendships. Learn the art of greeting people wherever you go. You will be welcomed everywhere.

Common Courtesies

Common everyday courtesies are taught in every school, but soon forgotten in adult life. The first is the use of the word 'please'. Just add 'please' to a sentence, and observe how quickly people respond. Every day, we say,

"Can I have it?" In return we get average service. When we say, "Can I have it, please?" the response is faster. To our request, we have added politeness, a symbol of fine breeding. Good service obviously follows.

We also learnt two simple words, "Thank you". We are shy of using them. Say "Thank you" to the little child who gives you a kiss; say it to the salesman who serves you on the sales counter. They will appreciate it. You will be treated better. "Thank you" conveys sincere gratitude. It conveys appreciation for service. Everyone is eager to be appreciated.

Two other words that we find difficult to use are "I'm sorry". They hurt the ego every time we use them. We were taught these words, but nobody told us that they could do wonders in our life. Whenever things go wrong, just say, "I'm sorry". The problem will be sorted out. Initially, it might hurt your ego, but soon you will realise that you have gained more than what you have lost. To accept one's fault is a sign of being a mature person.

Another two words that can do wonders for you are "Excuse me". Wherever you go if you find that the passage to your goal is blocked, just say, "Excuse me". You will find that your way is clear. To make what we say convincing, God blessed us with a smile. It costs nothing, but achieves much. Say it with a smile. The results will surprise you.

Think it over...

There is certainty of exquisite kindness and thoughtful benevolence in that rare gift – fine breeding.

— *Bulwer*

Using the Telephone

Nothing connects as many people together as the telephone. In a moment one can talk to people anywhere in the world. Homes and business houses now have internal exchange systems that connect everyone through telephones. Documents are transmitted through fax machines. Internet connected through the telephone has brought the world to every home. It has become possible to send messages and pictures and even chat with people around the world. A vast storehouse of knowledge is available through the Internet.

These developments have made it necessary to maintain etiquette and good manners on the telephone. A conversation on the telephone can make you happy and refreshed. On another occasion, it may arouse anger and hostility. It depends upon how you handle telephone calls. Here are a few things you will find useful to remember:

- A telephone is a device. Understand how it works. Learn how to use keys like mute, pause, flash and redial. Read the telephone booklet. Use the facility to store telephone numbers.
- One must maintain a personal telephone directory to record the names and telephone numbers of the persons one usually needs to speak to.
- For emergency use, the numbers of the hospital, fire brigade, railway station, the bus terminal, police station and your personal doctor must be on record.
- Use the telephone only when you need to. You must know whom you want to talk to and what you want to convey.

- When you get the dialed number, immediately disclose your identity by saying, "I am John. Could I please speak to...?" This way you have immediately conveyed who you are and whom you would like to speak to. If the person is available, he or she will come on line.
- When you dial a business number, the receptionist will greet you saying, "Good morning. This is ABC Ltd. Can I help you?" You could then disclose your identity and the person you would like to speak to. If you desire some information, the receptionist would connect you with the appropriate person.
- If the person is not available, the receptionist will request you to call later or leave your number.
- Telephones at railway stations and airports may be connected to a computer. Follow instructions to obtain the desired information.
- When you order food or groceries on the telephone, identify yourself, the address and the telephone number you are speaking from. To ensure that it is not a prankster, the service provider would ring back immediately to confirm the name of the caller and the order.
- When dialing international numbers, check the time of the country where you wish to connect the call. You could disturb the person at an odd hour.
- When speaking on the phone, it is your voice that creates an impression at the other end. Speak courteously. Be polite. Answer the call gently. Never use harsh language. While speaking on the phone, never converse with others simultaneously. Modern telephone instruments are sensitive. They pick up

voices from a distance. Sometimes it can create misunderstandings.

- Sometimes you may get a wrong number. Say "sorry" and close the call.

Think it over...

In conversation use some but not too much ceremony; it teaches others to be courteous, too. Demeanors are commonly paid back in their own coin.

— *Fuller*

Using the Mobile Phone

Mobile phones have linked people from the remotest areas of the world. It is necessary that one observes good manners and etiquette when using mobile phones. Here are a few guidelines about using mobile phones:

- People subscribe to mobile phone service for personal convenience. Do not impose upon others' privacy. Always try the landline number first. Dial the mobile phone number only in an emergency.
- Keep the conversation short and to the point. If the message is short, use SMS (short message service).
- Most people are guilty of disturbing people in restaurants, cinema halls and public meetings. Avoid this.
- Every day we hear phones ringing in public places. It is good manners to keep the ringer off when you are in public places.
- When speaking in a public place, speak softly to avoid disturbing others. If necessary, move to a

place where you can speak without disturbing others.

Carrying a mobile phone is useful when you are away from home. You can be traced in case of an emergency. You can call in case of need. It is dangerous to speak on a phone and drive at the same time. If it is urgent, stop the car and speak.

Using E-mail

With computers in every home, people send e-mails rather than write letters. This has cut down upon writing conventional memos and letters, but there is now the need to observe e-mail etiquette. It would be useful to follow these courtesies:

- Unless you check your mailbox every day do not give your e-mail address to everyone. It makes no sense if mail is not responded to.
- Write short messages in small case. Using 'all capitals' in the message is like shouting. Use this only when you need to shout at the recipient.
- When sending attachments, ensure that they are not large. They can choke the recipient's mailbox.
- Do not send any unsolicited mail. The recipient will not appreciate it.
- Do not pass e-mail addresses of your friends and acquaintances to others without their permission.
- Send mail only to concerned persons. Do not send copies to everyone you *think* would find the mail interesting.

- Do not indulge in creating chains or forwarding chain mail. No one was ever blessed by luck or received money by sending mails.
- Do not open attached mail received from persons you do not known. Many people have lost valuable data through virus received in the mail.

At Meetings

All kinds of meetings are held every day. In terms of manpower, these meetings cost large sums of money. Many of these meetings achieve nothing. When organizing or attending meetings, remember the following:

- Is the meeting necessary? A meeting must have a definite purpose to achieve.
- Has the meeting been properly announced? Have invitations been sent to all the participants? Has the agenda been circulated? Have appropriate arrangements been made?
- Meetings must start and end on time. One must respect other people's time. Discuss the agenda item-wise. The relevant material pertaining to the points of discussion must be available at the meeting.
- If there is a telephone in the room, disconnect it during the meeting. Request the participants to have their cell phones switched off.
- If refreshments are to be served, they must be served either before the meeting or after it. There should be no interruptions during the meeting.
- The minutes of the meeting must be recorded. They can be circulated later.

Public Meetings

Everyone needs to attend public meetings, as part of the audience or as a speaker, to introduce the speaker or present a bouquet to the chief guest. One could also be presiding over a public meeting. In each of these cases, one needs to maintain good etiquette.

As a part of the audience, one's responsibility is restricted to being a gracious guest. During the meeting one should not talk, use a mobile phone or walk around, disturbing others.

When presiding over a meeting, one's responsibilities begin before the meeting and ends when the guests have left. One must know the purpose of the meeting. Ensure that the physical arrangements are adequate. As the president, you will need to welcome special guests and brief them about the meeting. At the end, the president gives concluding remarks before the final vote of thanks.

When entrusted with the responsibility of introducing a guest speaker or presenting a bouquet or a garland, be prepared for it with the biodata of the guest or the bouquet or garland.

When invited to speak at a meeting, accept the assignment only if you have something special to say. Ask the organisers how long they expect you to speak. When speaking, keep within time. Water or refreshments should not be served during a speech. Handouts must be distributed after the speaker has finished speaking. It should be ensured that nobody disturbs the meeting with children running around or the audience speaking amongst them.

Thanksgiving at the end should be short. The purpose of thanksgiving is to say "thank you" to the guest speaker, the audience and others. It should not be an analytical commentary on what the speaker has said. That would be rude.

Think it over...

> Good breeding is the result of much good sense, some good nature, and a little self-denial for the sake of others, and with a view to obtain the same indulgence from them.
>
> — *Chesterfield*

Using the Road

Everyone needs to use roads. A road is a public place for everyone to use. Pedestrians and all kinds of vehicles use roads. Some vehicles move slowly. Others move fast. The slower vehicles must move on the left side and the faster ones on the right. In the interests of public safety many facilities have been devised. Many roads have been divided with a divider or a yellow line, and driving lanes have been painted. Traffic lights control the movement of traffic. Speed breakers, zebra crossings, overhead bridges or underground tunnels are provided. Take advantage of these provisions. They are conveniences devised for public safety. Follow these simple guidelines for safety on the road:

- Be acquainted with traffic rules. Follow them faithfully. The best safety device is a careful person.
- Walk cautiously on one side of the road. While crossing a road, first see towards the right side and

then towards the left side. Preferably cross at zebra crossings only.

- Maintain discipline on the road. Be polite to everyone.
- The slower vehicles must move on the left and the faster ones on the right.
- Give way to traffic on the right. Avoid overtaking.
- Slow down when you approach a light. Even if it is green, do not speed up to pass through before it turns red. It may turn red before you reach it.
- At a red light, stand in the appropriate lane.
- Drive in your lane. One who zigzags is a potential risk to self and others.
- Do not speed in the town. Speed thrills, but it also kills.
- Avoid driving close to buses and trucks. Allow sufficient place for buses to stop at designated bus stops.
- Drive slowly near schools, hospitals and through crowded markets and areas.
- Do not play loud music in the car. You may enjoy it, but it can prevent you from hearing a horn or signal. Besides, it disturbs others.
- Do not drink and drive. Drinking affects one's perception of speed and space. It also slows down reactions in emergent conditions.
- Do not use cell phones while driving. This divides your attention. It can also affect your emotions. This can cause an accident.

- When driving a two-wheel vehicle, use a helmet. In a car, use seat belts. If children are with you, ensure that they are secure in their seats.
- Always be courteous on the road. Even if the other person is at fault, give him the benefit of doubt. Avoid getting angry on the road.

Using the Highway

A highway is not like the roads within towns. While roads within towns join people and places together, a highway joins several villages, towns and cities together. Driving on the highway is different from driving within the city. The journey within the city is short. On a highway, the journey is long. The city roads are over-crowded. A highway is not. People move fast on the highway. Here are a few guidelines to follow:

- Keep vehicle speed within control. Safety is important.
- Always drive on your side. Avoid over-taking, especially on bends.
- Slow down when passing through villages and small towns. Beware of children and village folk not conscious of highway traffic.
- Do not brake suddenly. You could be hit by the vehicles following you.
- Maintain discipline at closed railway crossings. Line up on your side. Do not overtake waiting vehicles. One wrong move and the others follow.
- Drive carefully at night. Many trucks, tractor trolleys, and bullock carts move without a light. Many accidental deaths happen due to this single cause.

Parking Etiquette

Irresponsible parking is a matter of public concern. Millions of people are put to discomfort and inconvenience every day. Parking lots are provided in every town. They may be located at the railway station, the bus terminal, outside hospitals, hotels, schools, colleges, near markets, and other such places. At some places one needs to pay a nominal charge for the service. At other places, the service may be free.

To maintain parking etiquette, one needs to ask oneself a simple question, "Will my vehicle obstruct someone's passage and cause inconvenience?" If the answer is "yes", you are parking in the wrong place. Besides public convenience, one must also consider vehicle safety. Many places clearly indicate, "Parking at Owner's Risk." This implies that the parking attendant is not responsible for damage to the vehicle.

One may ride a bicycle, a scooter or motorcycle or a car. All need places to park their vehicles. Even public conveyances like *rickshaws,* taxis and buses need parking areas. However, nobody is entitled to cause inconvenience to others. For public convenience and safety certain areas are designated as "No Parking" areas or zones. Do not ignore these requests. Penalties can be imposed for breaking rules.

Think it over...

Good manners are a part of good morals; and it is as much our duty as our interest to practise both.

— *Hunter*

Visiting a Restaurant

Everyone needs to eat out in a restaurant sometimes. Generally, on arrival the steward welcomes and suggests an appropriate table. At peak times, the steward may request you to wait until a table is vacated. Please do not lose your "cool" on such an occasion. Here are a few guidelines to follow when visiting a restaurant:

- Most restaurants offer a *la carte* services. This means that you can choose the dishes from the menu card and pay for each dish. Sometimes a buffet spread is offered at a fixed price per person.
- The steward will inquire if you would like to order a drink. If you like soup, order that first. Some snacks can be ordered with the soup. If you do not want soup, you could directly order the meal. Servings are usually large. Generally, a mixed order is placed and dishes are shared.
- It is customary for the waiter to lay the table while the order is prepared. He will also place salad, pickle, chutney and ketchup to be had with the meal. When the dishes are brought in, the waiter may offer to serve everyone.
- After assessing the quantity, an additional order can be placed if required.
- To call the waiter during the meal, catch the eye of the nearest waiter or steward. It is discourteous to shout for him.
- The napkin is placed on the lap. Depending on the kind of food, it can be eaten with a fork and a knife, or a fork and a spoon. Items like *chapatti, naan*, bread, etc. that need to be eaten with the hand should be eaten that way.

- At the end of the meal, the waiter will bring warm water in a bowl to rinse the hands. Wipe them dry with the napkin.
- In some cultures, a crushed napkin is symbolic of a very enjoyable meal.
- During the meal, it is customary to place the cutlery with the tips of the fork and knife pointing at each other like the sides of the alphabet 'A'. On completing the meal, the cutlery is placed straight in the middle of the plate like the alphabet 'H'. The waiter will then clear the plate.
- The dessert is ordered after the meal.
- Once the meal is over you could ask the waiter for the bill. You can pay in cash or by credit card if it is acceptable. It is desirable that you should leave an appropriate tip for the waiter. Besides the tip, you could compliment the waiter for good service.
- If you are not pleased with the food, service or with a particular dish, do not get angry about it. Ask the waiter to call the steward. Pass your complaint to him in a businesslike manner.
- On your way out if the steward is at the door, you can just say, "Thank you" with a smile. Courtesy motivates everyone to serve well.

At a Club

It is commonplace for people to meet at clubs. Only members and their guests are entitled to use club facilities. Club members are bound by club rules. An elected managing committee administers the club.

Most clubs have a card room, billiard room, table tennis room, swimming pool, squash, and badminton and tennis courts. Clubs may also have a library and a reading room. Besides these, there will be a bar and a restaurant. Some clubs have residential rooms for guests. There are separate sets of rules for the use of these facilities. Members will necessarily need to be guided by these rules.

One meets and interacts with a variety of people in a club. To ensure good etiquette and manners, follow the simple rules of getting along with people. To be likeable, be humble. Everyone appreciates humility. Do not show off. Do not act pompous. Behave well with the members and the staff. A club is a joint property. Follow club rules. When aggrieved about any service, talk to the appropriate person. If your complaint is not attended, the matter could be referred to the managing committee.

Using Public Toilets

Everybody needs to use public toilets. We find them everywhere– at bus terminals, airports, in parks, trains, shopping plazas, restaurants and hotels. They are provided as a public convenience. Life would be difficult without them. Do we use them, as we should? Do we leave them clean and dry, as we would like to find them when we use them? Everyone wants to use them but does not care for their upkeep.

Simple rules apply for the use of public toilets. Use the urinal and toilet seats properly. Flush after use. If there is shortage of water, lodge a complaint about it. After using soap leave it in a soap dish or in a dry place. Do not leave the tap flowing. Do not spill water around the toilet seat. When people enter with dirty shoes, it leaves the toilet muddy. If you use toilet paper, carry some with you. It is not available in all public toilets. A little consideration on your part can make these public places more comfortable for everyone.

Places of Prayer

Depending upon personal faith people visit different places of prayer– temples, mosques, gurudwaras, churches, and others. Many homes have a place devoted to prayer. There is an equally big variety of religious customs and rituals. They may range from religious ceremonies at the birth of a child to *mundan* or sacred thread ceremony, or ceremonies at weddings, special remembrances and death. Each occasion requires certain etiquette to be maintained.

Most people consider footwear unclean. It is not permitted in places of prayer. In many places, as in gurudwaras and mosques, it is mandatory to cover the head. Some use a turban, others a cap or a scarf. One sits on the ground and should be appropriately dressed.

On most occasions your personal presence and attention may only be required. However, sometimes you may need to carry flowers, incense sticks, a coconut, sweets, and similar items for prayer. When in doubt, observe others. Look out for local customs and rituals. Follow others.

During the ceremony, observe self-restraint and silence. Do not disturb the ceremony or the people present at the ceremony. If *prasad* is served, accept it in your right hand supported by the left hand. If *tilak* is applied and you are not wearing a turban or cap, cover your head with the left hand.

When departing from a prayer meeting held in the memory of a deceased person, it is customary to meet the bereaved family with folded hands. Nothing needs to be said. Your expression should convey your sentiments.

Think it over...

Certain thoughts are prayers. There are moments when, whatever be the attitude of the body, the soul is on the knees.

— *Victor Hugo*

The Neighbours

Neighbours can be your best friends– and sometimes enemies too! It all depends upon the kind of relationship you wish to build with them. Follow these simple guidelines for better relationship:

- Accept your neighbours as good people. Only when personal self-interest interferes, problems begin to surface.
- Mind your own business. Do not step on each other's toes. Good relationships will develop naturally.
- Share happiness and not problems with neighbours. If there are problems of common interest, sit together and discuss how they can be resolved.

- If something went wrong because of your fault, apologise. Saying "sorry" should come as easily as saying "thank you".
- Co-operate with each other. Do not compete for petty things. Protect each other's interests. When you do a good deed, the neighbours will reciprocate.
- Gossip does the worst damage to good relations. Avoid gossip and criticism.
- Develop relationships with a positive attitude. A neighbour should be a friend who lives next door.
- Good etiquette and manners strengthen relationships between neighbours.

Gifts and Presents

A gift is a token of thoughtfulness for a person. It gives happiness to both, one who gives it and one who receives it. However, ill will is generated when people begin to assess and compare the value of a gift. A gift is a token of thoughtfulness. It need not be something that a person needs. Many people do not need anything. Should they not be given a gift? A gift reminds an individual of the emotional bonds of the person who has remembered you.

When one carries a bouquet of flowers to a sick person, it is not because the sick person needs it. His immediate need is medicine and medical care. Flowers cheer up a person. They reflect the glory of God. Their fragrance lifts up the spirits. Can any of these qualities be evaluated with money?

One should give with pleasure. One should receive with grace. Think of the sentiments of the person who thought and carried a gift for you. Gift-wrapping adds value to the gift. Do not skip on it – even if it is something for your wife or child. When you receive a gift, say "thank you" with a smile.

Smoking and Drinking

Smoking is prohibited in most public places. It is also prohibited in public conveyances like trains and buses. Many business houses also prohibit smoking in their premises. There are specific reasons for these restrictions. All smokers must observe them. When uncertain whether smoking is permitted, one must seek the permission of the persons in the vicinity. If smoking is permitted, it is simple courtesy to seek the permission of those accompanying you. Without your being aware of it, a person could be allergic to smoke. Elderly people are especially sensitive to this issue. Use an ashtray when you smoke. Put off the stub when you stop smoking. Do not leave it lit.

Social drinking is on the increase amongst men and women. It is considered fashionable to host cocktail parties. Some drink moderately. They stay within limits. A few drink indiscriminately and end up creating a nuisance for themselves and the hosts. Why is it that some people can drink a lot, yet remain sober? Some get tipsy even with small quantities. One must appreciate that alcohol is a drug. In small quantities, it can be beneficial. Like other drugs, the sensitivity to alcohol varies from one person to another. It would be difficult to assess what quantity would be right for anyone.

One should drink moderately. The hosts and the companions must feel comfortable. Unlike food, alcohol is absorbed in the stomach. It acts swiftly. One must drink slowly, sipping rather than gulping the drink. Initially, alcohol is stimulating. When the quantity of alcohol increases in the blood, it causes depression. This can cause a hangover the next morning. Do not let anybody force you to a drink. "One for the road" is a folly. You are drinking for pleasure. Do not let it become displeasure for you and others.

Points to Ponder...

- It is always a challenge to maintain good relationships with people.
- People are fun to those who find happiness with them.
- To understand people look at them from their point of view.
- To win people over make them feel wanted.
- There is no substitute for sincerity, integrity and honourable conduct in dealing with people.
- A greeting helps break the communication barrier.
- Common courtesies make life smooth and comfortable for everyone.
- One must maintain etiquette when using a telephone or mobile phone.
- Good meeting skills make a person welcome everywhere.
- Roads are for everyone to use. Always be courteous and understanding.

- Good etiquette and manners make visiting restaurants and clubs a pleasure.
- One must respect all places of faith and religion.
- Do unto your neighbours as you would want them to do unto you.
- Do not offend others with your smoking and drinking.

Pitfalls to Avoid

The ability to build and maintain good relationships with people has been a challenge to people throughout the history of mankind. Every age and generation has given us men and women who were able to suggest ways and means to attain our goal of understanding other people well. Most of these suggestions are documented, and they are available for us to learn from and use that knowledge to make life worthwhile.

Many truths and observations about mankind said thousands of years ago are as relevant today as they were when they were first spoken. The fact that this knowledge has passed from generation to generation and has not been trashed proves that it is useful. Yet mankind is as much at conflict with each other as it was thousands of years ago. Only a wise few have used the knowledge in their lifetime. The rest have lived in ignorance.

Has mankind always been foolish that it could not differentiate between what is good for it and what is not? Mankind's greatest weakness has been that everyone lives under a false notion: "I know what is best for me. Nobody in my circumstances can understand or handle the situation better." This false notion is enough to place a person on a pedestal like a statue that looks down at everyone but is unaffected by feelings and emotions of the people who surround it. People live with relationships of doubtful quality.

The scriptures of every faith and religion explain that both the good and the bad have existed at all times. There has always been a conflict between the two. Surrounded by confusion people suffer pitfalls in ignorance, damaging even the existing relationships. To avoid becoming a victim of such pitfalls, it would be best to be aware of them.

Lack of Self-control

Mankind's biggest tragedy has been the lack of self-control. Mankind has unfortunately undone the good work of others through lack of self-control. Man has ruined the gifts of nature because of selfishness. The ecology has been disturbed. The mountains have been eroded. The forests have been cut down. The rivers and lakes have been polluted. In greed, mankind has exploited everything. Even fellow brethren have not been spared. How can we then expect good relationships?

Everyone is a slave of his or her habits. A person is recognised as good or bad depending upon the balance between the good and bad habits. People say that nothing is good or bad, and it is only the thinking that makes it so. This is correct as what might be right in some cultures, may be objectionable in other cultures. Everyone has to live with one's own people and need to comply with whatever is desired and accepted in that group, community or country. Earlier we discussed about people being sensitive to certain things. Many of these sensitivities are based upon upbringing and family values. There are some that are universal. Let us consider some of them.

Rude Behaviour

Everyone values his or her self-esteem. Irrespective of one's age, status or position, everyone is sensitive when his or her self-esteem is attacked through rude behaviour. When people of high status and position tend to show that they are superior than others, most people resent such behaviour. It is a sure way to undermine any kind of relationship. Many "bosses" are guilty of this indulgence at the workplace.

Foul language and rude behaviour are not acceptable even by subordinates. No one likes to be humiliated. It is an insult to their self-esteem. Under such circumstances can a good relationship be made or maintained? Such behaviour can be likened to use of brute force through speech. Just as people resist physical brute force, they also resist verbal brute force. Out of necessity, some people may sometimes tolerate such behaviour. Eventually, the person is bound to hit back. A person who would like to maintain good relationships with people needs to be aware of this sensitivity in all people. One can build goodwill only through kindness and good behaviour.

Anger

Anger is a natural emotion. Everyone is bound to express it under certain circumstances. However, anger goes out of control very easily. When angry, a person uses language that is best avoided, utters words that are best unsaid. Besides, one may lose control over self. The face may turn red, the heartbeat becomes faster, the blood pressure soars, the mind becomes unsteady and the limbs tremble. One is prone to become violent. It could lead a person to a situation from where it is difficult to retreat.

Anger is a strong feeling of extreme displeasure. The cause of this displeasure could be a person or a situation. It could arise from a situation where one's desires are not fulfilled, and frustration may lead to anger. When it goes out of control, it no longer remains an outlet for frustration. It becomes a cause of serious concern.

Any person can easily become a prey to the pitfalls of anger. Life is full of provocative situations. Some people purposely create situations to cause provocation. The moment one is provoked, one loses one's temper and becomes angry, and the situation becomes one of disadvantage. When one reacts to a situation without sufficient self-control, it is bound to end in futility. Anger is natural, yet self-control is important for the positive use of anger. A person who desires to build and maintain good relationships must learn to handle anger with a positive attitude. This will help serve one's purpose well. It is difficult but not impossible.

Jealousy

Jealousy causes more heartburn amongst people than any other cause. To be jealous means to be envious of someone else's achievements or advantages. While it is all right to be protective of one's rights, privileges and possessions, the problem occurs when a person begins to compare trifling things with others. Jealousy emerges from self-doubt. A person may have all the facts, but jealousy clouds the mind to misinterpret them, arouse suspicion and even cause self-destruction. To be jealous is to poison oneself. Can anything else be worse?

A person who wants to maintain good relationships cannot afford to be jealous of others. That would be suicidal, an end to the journey towards the goal. One should not compare oneself with others. Everyone is unique. Everyone is different. Everyone attains what is in harmony with one's strengths and weaknesses. When everyone is different, would it be befitting to compare oneself with others? Everyone must accept oneself as a special person. Whenever in doubt, one must strive to remove the cause of the doubt. One must work to get ahead with all of one's ability. When a person is constantly striving to improve oneself, there is no cause for doubt or jealousy. One just gets ahead.

Revenge

Unfortunately, it is human nature to nurture a hurt and talk about it to malign the person who has caused it or to avenge it in one way or another. The feeling of revenge pushes the individual to hurt the other person equally. The majority does not see any harm in it because for them it is just tit-for-tat. They further argue that why should a person who has caused hurt not be punished? It apparently appears logical, but it is not always the best thing to do. Can you confidently say that the hurt was intentional? Are you sure that the person has not caused it in retaliation to something you might have done unintentionally? Would your response settle the score and bring back normalcy in your relationship? Honestly, the chances are that the person involved will drift apart. We see this happening every day in our homes, society and at the workplace.

A person who desires to build good relationships does not respond to a hurt through revenge. A more positive way is the path of forgiveness. In every religion of the world, we come across stories of good people who were laughed at, ridiculed and insulted. Sometimes, they were also physically hurt. Yet their response was never one of revenge. They always responded with forgiveness. To forgive, one needs to be emotionally mature, to rise above one's ego and offer a hand of friendship. It is something much more difficult to do than to reply in the same coin. They know that to keep touching a wound does not allow it to heal. The feeling of revenge has brought down families, communities and even nations. A person who desires to build good relationships is not an ordinary person. The person is willing to rise above trifling matters.

Think it over...

By taking revenge, a man is but even with his enemy; but in passing over it, he is superior.

— *Bacon*

Fallout of Success

Everyone desires success. Why should one not desire it? That is what everyone works for. While failure brings with it feelings of frustration, anger and jealousy, success too does not come alone. Success is accompanied with a feeling of elation, which gradually turns into pride, vanity and even arrogance.

It is natural for a person to be proud of one's success. It motivates one to work harder. The feelings that accompany it are important in that they motivate additional effort, which takes one towards additional successes. The danger does not lie in these feelings accompanying success, but in that these feelings tend to overcome individuals and gradually bring their success downhill. For a person who desires to build and maintain good relationships, it is not enough to succeed. To keep one's feelings under control is equally important. Let us examine them in a little more detail.

Pride

Success attracts recognition and applause. It is natural to feel elated on being recognised. This elation leads a person to pride. Appreciation and recognition are great motivating forces. Many successful people thrive upon them. Within limits pride motivates people. When in excess, people begin to resent it in a person. People are often heard saying, "He is too proud of his achievements to think of us." This is the beginning of the unmaking of a relationship. Should a person who desires good relationships risk it?

Pride is a deep pleasure or satisfaction gained from achievements, qualities or possessions. It also refers to self-respect. These are the positive aspects of pride. However, pride also means an excessively high opinion of oneself. This is the negative aspect of pride. When a person begins to hold an excessively high opinion of personal abilities, it is natural for others to resent it.

A person who desires to maintain good relationships must look at both the positive and the negative aspects of pride. Ruskin has wisely pointed out, "I have been more and more convinced, and the more I think of it, that, in general, pride is at the bottom of all great mistakes. All the other passions do occasional good; but whenever pride puts in its word, everything goes wrong; and what it might really be desirable to do, quietly and innocently, it is mortally dangerous to do proudly."

Vanity

Vanity is excessive pride in one's appearance or achievements. It also refers to the quality of being pointless or futile. Vanity is a step ahead of pride. It comes from the feeling that one is superior to others. The moment a person indulges in vanity, the others begin to feel inferior and small. And nobody likes that. Such a person soon loses the respect of friends and colleagues.

Vanity emerges from self-love, and one cannot totally avoid it. A person who wants to maintain good relationships needs to be cautious that it does not come as a pitfall that restricts growth. Personal compulsions and social needs oppose each other. Swift looks at vanity with a touch of humour, "The strongest passions allow us some rest, but vanity keeps us perpetually in motion. What a dust do I raise! Says the fly upon a coach-wheel. And at what a rate do I drive! Says the fly on the horse's back."

Arrogance

Arrogance is a step ahead of pride and vanity. A person becomes arrogant when he or she crosses the borderline between the positive and negative aspects of pride completely towards having a great sense of one's own importance or abilities. This leads to self-destruction. History has innumerable examples of people who were capable and possessed many good qualities, but arrogance led them to their end. World's best-known dictators fell because of arrogance. One negative quality overshadowed all the abilities and skills they possessed.

Arrogance emerges from over-confidence. Driven by passions rather than reason, over-confidence leads people to absurdities. Friends and colleagues never accept these kindly. The best of relationships turn sour. In extreme cases, arrogance leads to self-destruction. To avoid the pitfall of arrogance every person needs to be aware of the danger of nurturing pride, which leads the way to arrogance. If pride is kept under control and used only as a motivating force, a person grows. When it leads to negative behaviour, it rapidly helps arrogance grow. No person who desires good relationships can afford to let this happen.

Foul Language

The way people talk to each other depends upon their education, family background and respect for good behaviour. People who are not used to niceties of conversation may use words and phrases that are not readily appreciated or accepted in everyday life and for this reason the majority maintain very limited contact with such people. Even amongst educated people, we sometimes find that they let down courtesies of speech and use foul words and phrases that may arouse immediate objection. Good communication skills in people who desire to maintain good relationships require that the language used in conversation to be decent and respectful. Nothing puts off a person more than foul language one is not used to.

Think it over...

In the commerce of speech use only coins of gold and silver.

— *Joubert*

Vulgarity

It is not unusual for foul language to get vulgar even though it may be more to arouse humour than to offend the other person. If foul language is to be condemned, vulgarity in speech is still worst. Some people have the habit of being vulgar. They should not be surprised if people avoid them. One gets to see a lot of vulgar conversation particularly at stag parties, though one does get to see it even in parties where women and children are present. One would think that only men would indulge in vulgarity, but it is not so. Even women can be vulgar in their speech, much to the discomfort of men.

People who would like to maintain good relationships need to be aware of the pitfall of vulgarity in speech. It must be avoided at all times. Carlyle opines, "The vulgarity of inanimate things requires time to get accustomed to; but living, breathing, bustling, plotting, planning, human vulgarity is a species of moral ipecacuanha enough to destroy any comfort."

Obscenity

A step ahead of vulgarity one sometimes comes across yet another pitfall in obscenity, which has vulgarity mixed with indecent and disgusting sexual remarks. Both men and women are known to indulge in such profanities. Such conversation may be acceptable to a limited group, be it men or women, but it is taboo for a mixed group of people. Nothing puts off people as much as obscenity.

One may think that it does not exist, but it is not so. It exists at all levels of society. Films and television serials with gross sexual overtones has only confounded the problem. Children and young people are exposed to unnecessary viewing of the human body, many times highlighting the obscene. Magazines meant exclusively for men and women equally affect the society. These find their way to the young people also. With such exposure, it is not uncommon to hear obscene remarks in conversations. One who wants to maintain good relationships with people must be careful about these things. Anything obscene must be avoided at all times.

Insincerity

When people get to know one another, they begin to have certain expectations of each other. This is natural because getting closer means opening up to each other, expressing one's aspirations. It is hoped that the information that is exchanged during conversation will be held in sacred trust. It is also expected that when one speaks to the other one would mean what he or she says. These simple expectations are not unreasonable. And when one fails to fulfil them one should not be surprised to see the other person taking offence. One often wonders why people say something but mean something different.

Are they playing games? If so, why? The truth is that human relationships are fragile. People have strange likes and dislikes. With these, their attitudes and loyalties towards different people also change. Most people are unable to understand or appreciate human frailties. Their perception about most situations is superficial. Ill-equipped with knowledge, they take the support of insincerity to cope with certain issues and situations, not realising that sooner or later insincerity will come to the surface and the persons affected by it will take offence. A good relationship can be built only upon sincere behaviour and interaction.

The moment insincerity enters a relationship, it just snaps. Beware of this common pitfall.

Dishonesty

A step ahead of insincerity is dishonesty. One can be dishonest in many ways. Insincerity in speech is dishonesty. Misleading a person is also dishonesty. Cheating a person is another example of dishonesty. The worst is when people are dishonest, but they insist that they are honest. People can be dishonest with their spouse, children, friends and others. They can be dishonest at home, the workplace and in society. After indulging in dishonesty, people still wonder why they cannot maintain good relationships. They appear innocent about things going wrong.

People can be dishonest in speech, actions, at work and with money. People are also dishonest about their relationships. Some call it playing games with each other, but in reality it is dishonesty. Wherever truth, sincerity and a simple straightforward behaviour are missing in a relationship, it is plain dishonesty. Under such circumstances, one does not need to explain dishonesty. It becomes evident on its own. A person who needs to maintain good relationships should always avoid the common pitfall of dishonesty.

Breach of Trust

All relationships are based upon trust. To trust a person is to accept him or her as reliable, truthful, able, and possessing strength of someone or something. A child places trust in the parents just as they reciprocate it for the child. Friends trust each other. The employer places trust in the employees. If one were not to place trust upon each other, the society would collapse. We would all be loners.

People deposit their money in the bank because they trust it to offer security for the funds. What happens when we hear that a bank has run into serious trouble? People line up to withdraw their money. People lose their trust in the bank. This happens every day in financial circles. The moment a person or organization loses trust, people demand their money back. To be stable, one needs to maintain trust and goodwill of the people.

People establish trusts and foundations to look after different kinds of projects and services. Trustees who ensure that the work is efficient and effective manage these. When the trustees are careless, the organisation fails.

Good relationships are also maintained by placing trust upon each other. The moment this trust is breached, the relationship collapses. The breach could be as simple as letting out a secret, being insincere and dishonest or failing to comply with a responsibility inherent in the particular relationship. This could be between a parent and a child, between brothers and sisters or even amongst friends and colleagues. Sometimes it could also be a breach between an individual and the public at large. Professionals and clients may also separate because of breach of trust. This is a common pitfall where many people become victims. One who desires to maintain good relationships needs to be careful about it.

Think it over...

> Trust him little who praises all, him less who censures all, and him least who is indifferent about all.
>
> — *Lavater*

Physical Relations

With co-education in schools and colleges and men and women working together in offices, factories and other organizations, there is ample opportunity for both the sexes to interact with each other. With interaction, it is natural for a relationship to develop gradually with time. As long as these relationships are matter of fact and professional only, it is fine. However, when these relationships become intimate, the prospects of becoming a victim of this pitfall emerge strong and clear.

The majority may not agree that a danger lurks when men and women work together, but facts clearly point out that many fall an easy prey to this pitfall. Young people in schools and college do not realize that they are passing through adolescence, a critical phase of life. The hormones play their part and cause attraction between the sexes. Dating amongst young men and women is common. There are ample opportunities of being together. Unless the value system is strong, the young people cannot withstand the challenge of just being friends and not crossing the borderline. One can easily become a victim of this pitfall by indulging in a premarital sexual relationship. This is confirmed by the figures collected during surveys.

Young men and women working together are at a still greater risk of becoming victims of this pitfall because they are economically independent and may also be away from their parents who would have advised against such intimacy. Rather than get married, many couples experiment with live-in relationships, which apparently promise companionship and an outlet for the biological needs but are still free of the responsibility of making a home and raising a family. One is also spared of the pangs of divorce when the two may decide to separate. Superficially this sounds attractive, but it is not so. Such an arrangement is an intimate relationship similar to marriage, and when it fails, the injury and the hurt is no less than that of divorce. Besides, the society looks down upon it.

Even when the men and women are married, the danger of intimacy developing into a new relationship pulls a person towards this pitfall. Extramarital relationships are not new. They have always existed. However, today the pressures of getting involved in such relationships are stronger and more frequent. Only a strong value system that strengthens a family guards one against such relationships. Many of these relationships may be spontaneous and the result of thoughtless planning. These relationships may appear attractive, but they are a sure way of damaging one's marriage and existing relationships.

Another kind of relationship could be between a married man and a mistress or a married woman who may have a lover. In either situation, the persons may have their reasons for such a relationship, but the society looks down upon it.

With greater freedom for both men and women and with the option of expressing themselves openly, relationships between persons of the same sex are freely admitted. It is obvious that these people find some fulfilment in the relationship, but we cannot ignore that the society does not accept such relationships as normal.

We live in a society that has adopted certain customs and traditions, and in matters of physical relations our society accepts only marriage between a man and a woman. In different cultures and in a variety of circumstances, people may develop relationships that are not readily accepted by the society. A person who respects the ethics and morals of the society will need to live only by the relationships that are accepted by it. The moment a person steps out of these relationships one is ready to become a victim of this pitfall.

Controversies

People have very strong opinions about certain issues in life. The moment the issue comes up, they cannot resist speaking emphatically about it. Since others are equally at liberty to express their opinion, it is not long before there is a debate. Since there is no judge, nobody wins. Everyone who joins the debate gets the matter off the chest, feeling relieved that he or she has had his or her say. One quietly feels elated for having put forward very valid arguments.

Did it make any difference to the person who had opposing views? Not in the least. Arguments do not always convince or change people. They only lead to strained or broken relationships. We see it happening every day. A couple may argue amongst themselves, teenagers may argue with their parents, a quarrelsome subordinate may argue with the boss and a customer may argue with a shopkeeper. Arguments are the foundation of all controversies. A person might feel happy about winning an argument. But one cannot be happy for losing a friend or severing an otherwise good relationship.

A person who needs to build and maintain good relationships cannot afford to get into controversies. One must always withdraw from an unnecessary argument, be it at home, the workplace or in society. One must understand that it is not possible to change people by expressing your views, however strong and valid they may be. A person will not change unless one is personally willing to do so. To change people, one needs to be in harmony with them on points of common agreement and not to get into a controversy with them. A person who desires to maintain good relationships must steer clear from all kinds of controversies.

Think it over...

Most controversies would soon be ended, if those engaged in them would first accurately define their terms, and then adhere to their definitions.

— *Tryon Edwards*

Attachment

All faiths and religions explain that attachment is the cause of all sorrows and grief. Everyone comes to this world alone and departs from it alone. The relationships one develops with wealth and people are temporary, to be left behind at death. Parents give birth to children and bring them up, making great sacrifices in the hope that in the old age they will support them. But it rarely happens that way. Mostly the children leave their parents when they get involved with a family of their own.

Attachment makes a person subjective. It promotes desires. When these desires are fulfilled, one desires even more. When some of the desires are not fulfilled, one feels frustrated. This frustration leads to anger, which further leads to jealousy and revenge. These negative emotions cloud one's thoughts, leading one to still greater negative reactions.

Under such circumstances is it right to be attached? People argue that it is natural to be attached to one's wealth, spouse, children and family. It might be natural because it is instinctive. But at the same time, it is the cause of sorrow or grief. To rise above attachment, one needs to adopt the attitude of a trustee where one fulfills one's responsibilities without being attached. When one looks at the wealth and relationships as a trustee, one does the best by doing what is expected. At the time of a loss, one accepts it as the will of God.

A person who desires to maintain good relationships must look at life as a trustee who has limited privileges and responsibilities. One must fulfil these happily without any form of attachment.

Being Judgmental

Some people have a comment to make about everyone and everything. They are know-alls, perched up on a pedestal passing a judgment on one and all. They enjoy doing it and feel elated about being superior to everyone. Do these people enjoy good relationships? Of course, not! Nobody likes to be criticized or commented about. Nobody likes to be made to feel small. The more they indulge in it, the lower the esteem they enjoy.

A person who desires to maintain good relationships must avoid showing off one's knowledge or ability. One should not make comments or criticize others. Even when it is necessary to find fault and show the right way, it must be done in a positive way so that the other person does not take offence. A person's consideration in these matters is well appreciated. When a person is knowledgeable, it does not mean that the knowledge should be used to show down another person. A positive way is to share knowledge. Rather than criticize a mistake, it would be better to suggest simply by saying, "Would it not have been better if you did it in such and such a way?" This way you tell the other person that there is a better way of doing it, yet not cause offence.

Seeking Favours

Many people are good at turning acquaintances into friends, but soon lose out when they seek favours of these people. A certain amount of give and take is normal amongst friends and relations, but some people like to seek favours from everyone. One must remember that doing favours and seeking them is like depositing or withdrawing money from a bank. When you do a favour, it is like depositing the value of the favour in the bank. Similarly, when you seek a favour it would be like withdrawing the value from the bank. If you withdraw too much, it becomes an overdrawn bank account and nobody would appreciate that. A person who wishes to build good relationships through goodwill, favours others and seeks a favour only in an emergency and not as a habit.

Think it over...

We are always much better pleased to see those whom we have obliged, than those who have obliged us.

— Rochefoucauld

Lending and Borrowing

Shakespeare advises, "Never a lender nor a borrower be because a loan loses both itself and friend." There is great wisdom in this advice. People will repeatedly confirm its validity. Almost everyone has been a victim of this pitfall in life, either as a lender or a borrower. Everyone will agree that it is easy to lend money, but difficult to recover it. Those who are in the lending business have their own tough ways to recover the loans.

Some people still borrow from friends, but a vast majority borrows from banks and financiers. While businessmen appreciate the need for fiscal discipline and observe rules, borrowers who buy almost all of their needs on hire-purchase terms are often guilty of breaking the rules and getting embarrassed about it. One needs to live within one's means. Many luxury items are made available on hire-purchase terms, but just because they are available it does not mean that one should buy them, particularly when they are used only occasionally. While the loss from an unrecovered loan is a personal loss, the embarrassment from failure to repay a loan damages one's credibility and good relationships forever.

Points to Ponder...

- Most people suffer pitfalls in ignorance, damaging existing relationships.

- Lack of self-control has been mankind's greatest weakness.
- Rude behaviour amounts to using verbal brute force.
- Anger out of control is a cause of serious concern.
- Jealousy causes more heartburn than any other cause.
- To maintain relationships, a person must rise above trifling annoyances.
- Successful people must keep pride within control, lest it takes the shape of vanity or arrogance.
- One cannot maintain relationships in the presence of foul language, vulgarity and obscenity.
- Insincerity and dishonesty cannot be hidden from people for long.
- All relationships are based upon mutual trust.
- The society does not accept physical relationships that do not have the sanctity of law.
- To maintain relationships one must avoid controversies at all times.
- Attachment is the cause for sorrows and grief.
- Never judge others lest they judge you.
- Those who receive more than what they give can never build good relationships.

Making Lasting Relationships

Moving step by step we have, observed that while some relationships are built naturally through birth into a family, there are many others that need to be built as one goes through life. We have also observed that making relationships is difficult for several reasons. Maintaining them is even more difficult. We have also considered the different kinds of relationships one builds during the lifetime– within the home, the workplace and the society. We have also discussed the possible pitfalls that restrict the building and maintaining of good relationships.

What then should be the next step in making lasting relationships? Is it worthwhile to put in the effort to make and maintain these relationships? Aren't relationships full of stress and tension? Aren't they a source of heartbreak also? People seek the answers to these questions and many more. Everyone knows that making and maintaining relationships is a difficult task. It requires one to possess the skills to be able to get along well with a variety of people. These skills are very valuable. Those who possess them are sought by everyone and occupy high positions in every field.

Like other abilities people need to learn the skills that help one get along with others. Unfortunately, these skills are not like the physical skills that can be mastered quickly. These skills include the understanding of the human mind and behaviour. With everyone being different, it is not an easy task. Several fields of specialisation have emerged in this pursuit. It is for an individual to interpret the information and knowledge from one's personal point of view. This can involve a lifetime of effort and experience. Once a person sets out to develop skills to deal with people, one gradually develops an insight into the human behaviour and gradually attains the goal.

Building Relationships

A relationship is built upon mutual attraction and cooperation between two people. It may begin with two people meeting each other in a particular situation and becoming acquaintances. A chance meeting leads them to know each other. The next step could be the development of a liking for each other. This liking could gradually become intense, and they would begin to offer support to make each other. A mutual relationship has been created. The intensity of this relationship would eventually depend upon mutual interaction between the two. The relationship could be deep and lasting, or it could be shallow, superficial and temporary.

What is it that from being acquaintances two persons begin to like each other? What is it that makes this liking develop into a relationship? It could simply be that they share common interests. It could also be that similar vibrations emerge from them, and they are naturally attracted towards each other. It could also be that the two share similar feelings, and these in turn influence the emotions in each other.

An emotion is defined as a strong feeling. It could also mean an instinctive feeling as distinguished from reasoning. The word 'emotion' originated from the Latin *emovare* meaning 'disturb'.

Psychologists tell us that there are three distinct factors that influence emotions. First, what arouses an emotion? Second, how do the body and the mind respond to the arousal? And third, how do the physical and mental reactions influence the emotion? While these three factors have been identified, it is not possible to exactly understand emotions because biorhythms and hormones also influence the body. The conscious mind may react quickly to particular circumstances, but eventually the results would depend upon an individual's thought and memory processes that depend upon past experiences.

Most young people are not exposed to sufficient experiences to be able to evaluate their own feelings and emotions. Due to lack of emotional maturity, they rely more upon how they feel at a particular time rather than understand that their body could be misleading the mind and the relationships. Emotional growth does not come automatically. It is dependent upon one's ability to interpret information and experiences to personal benefit. This, in turn, depends largely upon the values one learns in childhood. One matures emotionally with the coming of stability in one's thoughts and actions. This is an individual process. While some mature early, there are others who may have to wait for a long time.

When two acquaintances begin to like and support each other, it could be said that a new relationship is born.

One could also say that a relationship is built when two persons are able to reach out to each other's emotions.

Factors Influencing Relationships

Several factors influence the making and maintaining of relationships. Since people react differently to these factors, everyone is eager to know what would be the best way to handle the situation. It is not easy to answer this question because men and women may respond in a variety of ways at different times. The best thing to do would be to understand how people influence each other to develop and benefit from relationships. Let us consider some of them.

Money: Everyone is fully aware of how people use money to influence each other. Money is symbolic of power. It has a great motivating force. It is used at home, the workplace and in society to influence and motivate people. It is not always honestly earned. Yet most people would do anything to obtain more money.

Many relationships are built around money. Money means greater purchasing power and security. It promotes greed but ensures comfort. It tests one's honesty and integrity, and many a times people ignore their conscience and values for it. Everyone needs money for survival, but when people make money their God, they are heading for trouble. Money is a good slave, but a poor master. Use it only for positive purposes to build relationships.

Think it over...

Put not your trust in money, but put your money in trust.

— *O.W. Holmes*

Position: Many are attracted to people who hold special positions. Again, this may be at home, the workplace or in society. People respect position and seek to build relationships with people of high positions in the hope of taking advantage whenever possible. Within a family, a person tries to please the head of the household to seek favours in times of need. At the workplace, who does not want to please the boss? It means smooth sailing at work. Even in the society people build special relationships with key people at all levels to make life comfortable and easy. One needs to handle these relationships with care.

Personal needs: A person's needs could compel him or her to build relationships. These needs could be as diverse as a person desiring spiritual growth and building a relationship with an able guru, who could guide one towards the goal, or a weak and needy person desiring economic security to build a working relationship with a person who is financially sound. Circumstances lead individuals to build relationships in strange ways, many a times even against their will. However, we need to remember that a person's needs could be a vital factor in building a relationship.

Love and care: Some people are kind, courteous and caring towards others who cannot help but like them. This often leads to building a large circle of admirers, who desire a two-way relationship on long-term basis with these people. Kindness and courtesy come naturally to a virtuous person. They spread the message of goodwill wherever they go. There could be no better way to develop relationships than to follow the path of building goodwill at all levels of life – at home, the workplace and in society.

Personal attraction: People are attracted to persons who exude charm and goodwill. Everyone wants to build a relationship with such a person. This charm may or may not be inherited. A personality that is truly attractive is built upon a virtuous life and a realization of the power that lies within every individual. This power has to be developed through effort and perseverance. Once developed, it helps build positive relationships in life.

Developing an Attractive Personality

People are automatically attracted to a person with an attractive personality. Observe people carefully. Some are more attractive than others. This attraction is not physical only because that would be superficial. Good clothes and grooming help make one attractive, but this attraction holds one's attention for a brief period only. The real attraction comes from qualities that are deep-rooted and developed over years of effort and perseverance. Let us consider some of the important factors that make one more attractive.

Character: One's character makes a person unique. The power that comes from character knows no boundaries of colour, caste or creed. It is not limited to one's financial resources either. It easily overshadows the possessions of riches, knowledge, intellect or genius. A person's character refers to what a person believes in. The power from one's character comes from being responsible, conscientious, truthful and honest. All religions aim at teaching the same thing. The simple truths are described in different forms and illustrated with lives of men and women to make the arguments convincing. One cannot build character overnight. It is the accumulated result of good deeds done in everyday life until they become a part of the person. In time of need, one can draw upon this strength because it lies deep within.

Conscience: We seek God in temples, mosques and churches. We seek Him in places of pilgrimage. We seek Him everywhere and forget to look within where He resides at all times. God resides within us as our conscience. We shape our conscience with our character. We fail to experience the pleasure of God within us because we ignore virtues like patience, tolerance, kindness and benevolence, and give in to impatience, greed, anger, jealousy and hatred. Can God be pleased with us? The practise of simple virtues gradually adds on great power to a person. One builds the character, and at the same time prepares the conscience to provide answers to difficult situations in life.

Communicating with God: Communicating with God through prayer helps us to convey our gratitude for every little thing we are blessed with. Unfortunately, all of us give greater importance to what we do not have rather than to what we do have. Which one of us should not be grateful for being blessed with a healthy body, two legs to walk about with, two hands to work with, two eyes to see everything, two ears to hear everything and above all else a mind to think for ourselves? Is anyone of us willing to think of life without these blessings? Which one of us is willing to part with any of these blessings for some money, comfort or luxury?

To be attractive to people, learn to communicate with God through prayer and meditation. To pray simply means to talk to God in your own way. Thank Him for what He has blessed you with. Talk to Him about your problems. He will respond. To meditate means to think fully and deeply about your self. The word 'meditation' is derived from the Latin root meaning "to heal". Meditation makes us feel better. We begin to understand the futility of our desires and our greed. We begin to seek true knowledge based upon a virtuous life. Meditation takes us deep within to introspect about our thoughts and feelings and connect with the God within. Even the brief moments of communication bring great happiness. This gradually grows into bliss.

Charisma: Charisma refers to the charm that inspires admiration and enthusiasm in other people. Those who possess a personality that attracts immediate attention are said to be charismatic. It is believed that charisma is a gift of nature or a divine favour. Such people are able to charm, inspire, persuade and influence others, which helps acknowledge them as natural leaders. It has been observed that charismatic people experience emotions strongly. They are enthusiastic and make others feel enthusiastic too. They feel strongly about what they desire to attain and let nothing obstruct them.

Although it is popularly believed that charisma is a gift of God, it has been observed that charisma can be developed like other qualities in human beings. When actors can act charismatic on stage or on screen, why can a person not develop it through study and effort? With development of the personality, there is a gradual rise in personal charm, which helps to make and maintain good relationships.

Communication skills: Unless a person can communicate well, it is not possible to build good relationships. Communication is the act or process of communicating, the imparting or exchanging of thoughts, opinions or information. It also refers to something imparted, interchanged or transmitted. In general, it refers to the use of speech or writing, as is done through verbal or written messages. Many people are known to draw attention through their writing skills. Similarly, one who has an attractive voice and can communicate ideas by developing good public speaking skills attracts others easily. People also communicate through body language. Much is communicated without a word through clusters of gestures, some voluntary and others involuntary. Clothes, grooming and one's actions also help in communicating to attract attention and making relationships. It was not recognised earlier, but people also communicate by way of generating both positive and negative vibrations that influence others nearby. Good communication skills help develop lasting relationships.

Consideration for others: Have you ever observed how quickly people are attracted towards those who are considerate and courteous? When a person says, "May I help you?" one immediately accepts the person being worthy of personal interaction. Domestic help, taxi drivers, salesmen in stores, airhostess in planes and others in different spheres of life win over one's confidence immediately when they offer to help and serve.

Here is a lesson one needs to learn from them. One who desires to build good relationships must always be considerate and thoughtful about others. Etiquette and good manners help to smooth out life. A helpful attitude draws other people closer, gradually transforming into a regular relationship. Business houses that offer the best service to their customers rise quickly and are always the first choice of the customers.

Love

All young people are fond of talking about love. They will tell you that love is a many splendoured thing. While they are ecstatic talking about love, the parents wish that their children could understand the meaning of "love" better. They emphatically insist that the young people might be attracted towards each other; that they probably "like" each other. But the young people insist that it is "love". The word "like" in terms of affection means the experience of happiness, felicity, bliss, enchantment, ecstasy or something similar in the presence of another person. These experiences come from harmony between two people. Love is a much deeper emotion.

Once a person starts liking another person, one begins to develop an affection, fellow feeling, fondness, admiration, regard, goodwill, adoration and devotion for the other person. One begins to look at the other person with a new perspective. This is certainly a step ahead of liking a person. Yet, it is not love. Love is a far deeper emotion than most people would accept. There is an element of selfishness in a person's affections, or what they call "love". True love is selfless.

Arthur Schopenhauer, the renowned German philosopher, called "love" an illusion. What a young man and woman ecstatically drawn towards each other call "love" may be the force of nature drawing the two together to propagate the human race. The couple feel that they are finding great happiness from their "love" for each other, but it may only be an illusion in that nature has drawn one towards the other to keep the human race going. When nature's purpose is fulfilled, the "love" wanes.

Love is not a spontaneous reaction in a relationship. In comparison, attraction and liking are spontaneous reactions. One can be attracted to a person. One could also like a person readily. Love is different. It does not come spontaneously. It must develop gradually. It has to be learnt because it is difficult to understand. True love means giving a part of yourself– unconditionally!

Love is an emotion that encourages intelligent self-expression in the partner and creates an atmosphere where the two can find greater happiness together than each could find separately. True love encourages a person. Encouraging is giving. Here it is giving an opportunity for intelligent self-expression, which is indeed a positive thing to do. It further creates an atmosphere where the two can be happy together. The emphasis is on mutual happiness and not on individual happiness. Such love can surely not be spontaneous. It can only develop gradually when two persons share similar hopes, aspirations and goals with the determination to face individual fears and problems together. Such a love is the result of mutual trust, respect and consideration.

In everyday life when young people talk of "love", there is an element of expectation or benefit from the relationship. As long as that expectation is fulfilled, the "love" lasts. When that expectation is not fulfilled, the "love" ends and feelings of frustration, anger, conflict, indifference and even hatred rise in their heads. This "love" is based upon ignorance, attachment, desire and passion. For "love" to rise to a higher plane, one needs to draw from the inner forces, which are detached from selfishness.

To experience the positive feelings of "love", it is easier when it is directed towards God. When this kind of love is shifted to a person, it does not get mixed up with other considerations that may overshadow it. Such love is based upon the higher values of life, and it draws strength from within, from the heart and the mind.

Think it over...

Let grace and goodness be the principal loadstone of thy affections. For love, which hath ends, will have an end; whereas that which is founded on true virtue, will always continue.

— *Dryden*

Other Virtues

While the majority believes that relationships are made when people like or love each other, the truth is that relationships are made when a person is virtuous. Some of the common virtues that make people attractive are patience, tolerance, courtesy, kindness, friendliness, sincerity, truthfulness, honesty, moderation, flexibility, forgiveness, generosity, thoughtfulness, being charitable, merciful and benevolent, conscientiousness, purity, devotion, humility, persistence and steadfastness. One virtue leads to another. When a person is virtuous, it is natural to emit positive vibrations.

Love leads one to respect, gentleness, cooperation, mercy, compassion, generosity and benevolence.

Patience, tolerance and serenity make one peaceful. Simplicity and humility promote self-respect. Happiness is expressed through humour, laughter and cheerfulness. Honesty and truthfulness go hand in hand. Knowledge promotes self-confidence, courage and wisdom. All these virtues make a person attractive to make relationships.

Everyone admires virtuous people. It is not for nothing. It takes great effort to be virtuous. Patience is a simple virtue. However, it is not easy to practise patience because it requires great self-control. It requires one to accept people as they are. Tolerance requires one to accept something that one does not like. Again, this is not easy. One needs to have a lot of self-control to practise tolerance. Very often persons who are patient and tolerant are considered weak. In reality, they are strong in that they possess great self-control to practise these virtues.

It is natural for a person to retaliate when some wrong is done. Anger and revenge come easily. However, it is very difficult to practise forgiveness. It is not easy to forgive someone who has cheated or betrayed one. Forgiveness requires one to rise above a natural reaction and act magnanimously. While retaliation is a negative response, forgiveness is a positive step to heal an injured relationship.

Humility, the quality of being humble, means that one should not entertain the feeling of self-importance. It requires one to rise above one's ego, to be free from "I", "me" and "mine". This requires one to live a detached life, to give up the feeling of possessiveness. It is difficult to practise, but it is only through humility that one rises to angelic heights.

To be virtuous one needs to accept high moral values in life. Make a list of all the virtues you would like to inculcate in your life. Paste this list at a place so that you can see it every day. Dedicate each day to practise one virtue. For example, on the first day you could practise patience. Throughout the day keep reminding yourself that you will be patient, happen what may. Practise patience at home, the workplace and wherever you go. In the evening, evaluate your own performance. Where did you go wrong? Why? How? Could it have been avoided? In the same way, practise tolerance the next day. Follow the same procedure culminating with evaluation in the evening. In a week you would have practised seven different virtues. Repeat the process over the next week. With conscious effort and practise you will begin to experience a positive change in your personality. As a more positive person, you will be able to develop better relationships in every sphere of your life.

Think it over...

Wealth is a weak anchor, and glory cannot support a man; this is the law of God that virtue alone is firm, and cannot be shaken by a tempest.

— *Pythagoras*

Listen More Talk Less

People avoid those who talk more than they listen. Human nature is such that people want a willing ear to hear their woes and their achievements, and not talk to them about their own affairs. This may appear to be an unfair demand. But this is how it is. The person who wants to build relationships needs to be a good listener.

Most people are not good listeners. When one has a goal to attain which depends upon listening skills, it becomes necessary to acquire these skills. This will help one to build better relationships. Listening effectively is an acquired skill. It requires one to concentrate on what is being said. One can listen almost at four times the speed one speaks. Because of the gap, the listener is tempted to interrupt and agree or disagree with whatever is being spoken. To be a good listener, it is necessary that one must refrain from speaking until the other person has finished speaking. Sometimes, even when the listener does not interrupt, the mind may stray to other thoughts, and one fails to comprehend the message.

To listen effectively, one must sit straight with an erect back. This enhances attentiveness. Next, the listener must have an eye contact with the speaker. When the two look at each other, there is an unsaid assurance that one is listening. The process of listening begins with the hearing of the message correctly. Then it should be interpreted and understood from the correct perspective. The next obvious step is to evaluate it and form an opinion about it. If the message is useful, it can be stored for future use. To assure the speaker that the message has been received in the correct perspective, it must be appropriately acknowledged.

Socrates has rightly reminded us, "Nature has given us two ears, two eyes but one tongue, to the end that we should hear and see more than we speak." If extraneous thoughts invade the mind when listening, one should remind oneself the importance of what is being said. Remind yourself that the information is important to you. People are attracted to those who lend a willing ear, and it becomes possible to build good relationships.

Relationships and Stress

It is always stimulating to meet new people and build relationships. However, one soon tires of a person and a certain amount of anxiety and stress begin to build. With some people this stress builds up faster, with others it might be slow. Similarly, some people do not get anxious or experience stress when interacting with people, while others do so they avoid excessive interaction with people. This only means that people react differently to their relationships with people. Keeping this in view, most persons choose people and circumstances that are in harmony with their temperament.

People adopt all kinds of ways to cope with stress that arises from different kinds of relationships. Few women realise that their nagging is looked down upon just as one would avoid men who are always judgmental. People who are calm and patient cause the least amount of stress in others and are always welcome. On the other hand, all aggressive men and women are avoided.

One must remember that there is no such thing as perfect people. We are not perfect, and we cannot expect others to be perfect either. To ensure that a relationship is free of stress, one must not try to find fault or change people. Instead, one should try to find out areas of agreement that would strengthen the relationship. Every person needs his or her own privacy and space, and this right must always be honoured. When a relationship is positive and seeks only the good and common interests in each other, it gradually builds up.

To ensure a stress-free relationship, here is a list of things to remember. Everyone has the right to:

- think and behave in whatever way one likes.

- make mistakes and learn from them.
- be responsible for what one does and not give any explanations.
- be what one likes to be and refuse to accept what others want one to be.
- ask questions; the other is free to refuse an answer.
- learn only what one wants to.
- not to be responsible for others' problems.
- react to situations and circumstances in one's own way.
- seek silence, privacy and space.
- follow the faith and religion one likes.

Conflict – Management and Resolution

When anxiety and stress from a relationship go out of control, we have an unhappy situation. It could be described as a situation of conflict. If not correctly managed or resolved, it could result in a broken relationship, which could cause hurt to one or both the parties, sometimes affecting many other people.

One needs to understand that relationships are not toys to play with and to throw away when one has had his fill. We cannot overlook that human relationships are complex. They involve the feelings and emotions not only of the persons who are directly involved, but sometimes also of those who are connected with them. Important considerations at the workplace might be at risk. Problems could be complicated, difficult to understand, and therefore finding an immediate solution might be difficult.

Most conflicts arise from the breakdown of effective communication. When one of the persons feels that there is no solution to the conflict, the situation becomes worse. Some of the common reasons for breakdown in relationships include use of coarse language, lack of etiquette and good manners, physical abuse, drug and alcohol addiction and betrayal. To resolve a problem, one must look at it objectively. The moment a person becomes subjective the problem is confounded.

When things go wrong and the situation becomes difficult, one should ask oneself some questions rather than blame the other person. Am I committed to the relationship? Have I looked at the situation from the other person's point of view or am I taking a one-sided view? Are my expectations from the relationship realistic? Am I as much concerned about the other person's happiness as much as I am about myself? Have I contributed my share in maintaining the relationship as the other person? Could I make amends to maintain the relationship? Am I ready to take the few extra steps that I expect the other person to take? Am I selfish in my relationship? If so, what am I doing about it? The answers to these questions will easily lead one to a solution.

Think it over...

Man perfected by society is the best of all animals; he is the most terrible of all when he lives without law, and without justice.

— *Aristotle*

Relationships are Like Sand

The wise draw our attention to yet another truth. They tell us that relationships are like sand. When you have your palm open, you can hold a small mound of sand on it. As you close the fist the sand trickles through the fingers leaving only a few grains locked up. Like sand, one can make and maintain many relationships as long as one is open in mind and spirit like the palm. When one closes one's mind and adopts a strict attitude very much like the closing palm, the relationships slip out of hold and are no longer tenable.

To make and maintain relationships, one needs to have an open mind, a willingness to accept people as they are and to enjoy them as unique individuals and not as one in the crowd. People who are outgoing, flexible and have an open mind and ears to listen to others always build relationships quickly. The secret lies in the attitude and not in technique.

Relationships are Impermanent

One needs to remember that no relationship is permanent. Even the most primary relationship between a mother and a child is some day broken when one of the two leaves the other, or dies. This way all relationships are impermanent. All that one can do is to enjoy a relationship as long as it lasts. The longer it lasts the better it is.

In the *Ramayan,* it is said that when Lakshman returned after leaving Sita in the forest, he went straight to Sri Ram who sat dejected and heart broken. Circumstances had compelled Sri Ram to live apart from Sita. Touching Sri Ram's feet, and with his hands folded in respect, Lakshman said, "As directed by you I have left

Sita at Valmiki's holy hermitage by the river Ganga. Perhaps destiny has so decreed. Please do not grieve at being separated from Sita. The wise and the noble do not feel dejected. We gather only to distribute. We rise only to come down some day. We unite only to separate. Separation is imminent through death. Therefore, attachments to the spouse, the children, friends and wealth are always painful even though we know that separation is certain. Why then are you given to sorrow?"

It is natural to grieve and feel heartbroken when a relationship breaks. However, it is important to understand that all relationships are impermanent and have to end. Attachment increases one's grief and sorrow, and the wise advise against it. When making relationships, one must remember this plain truth. Relationships are there to enjoy as long as they last. Do unto others as you would want them do unto you. When you express care and concern for others, it comes back to you manifold.

Think it over...

The gods conceal from men the happiness of death, that they may endure life.

— *Lucan*

Points to Ponder ...

- An understanding of the working of the human mind and behaviour helps develop and maintain relationships.
- All relationships are built upon mutual attraction and cooperation.

- Several factors like money, position, personal needs, and love and care influence everyday relationships.
- An attractive personality emerges from a noble character, the conscience and respect for the divine.
- Love is more often misunderstood than understood.
- The true value of a person lies in the virtues one is able to develop and use in life.
- Good listening skills help build good relationships.
- Interaction with people sometimes causes stress. One must learn to cope with it.
- Conflicts must be managed and resolved tactfully.
- People with open minds and hearts develop and maintain many relationships.
- All relationships must end some day. Enjoy them while they last.